CW01018605

A REASON TO RHYME

Edited by

Heather Killingray

First published in Great Britain in 2001 by
POETRY NOW
Remus House,
Coltsfoot Drive,
Peterborough, PE2 9JX
Telephone (01733) 898101
Fax (01733) 313524

HB ISBN 0 75432 712 4
SB ISBN 0 75432 713 2

FOREWORD

Although we are a nation of poets we are accused of not reading poetry, or buying poetry books. After many years of listening to the incessant gripes of poetry publishers, I can only assume that the books they publish, in general, are books that most people do not want to read.

Poetry should not be obscure, introverted, and as cryptic as a crossword puzzle: it is the poet's duty to reach out and embrace the world.

The world owes the poet nothing and we should not be expected to dig and delve into a rambling discourse searching for some inner meaning.

The reason we write poetry (and almost all of us do) is because we want to communicate: an ideal; an idea; or a specific feeling. Poetry is as essential in communication, as a letter; a radio; a telephone, and the main criterion for selecting the poems in this anthology is very simple: they communicate.

CONTENTS

CHANCE ROMANCE

I'm a gambler,
Quite mendacious,
Who plays emotions,
Efficacious,
While I win I'm in your heart,
Though when I lose I fall apart,
But when I'm on a winning streak,
We have such times most unique,
Though when I'm losing,
Often boozing,
We're always choosing the wrong time to speak.

Anthony John Ward

A SONG FOR YOU

I haven't a 'bicycle made for two',
I haven't a 'golden frame'.
But 'I belong to Glasgow'
'And just like the ivy, I'll cling to you'.

'With someone like you'
With 'two eyes of blue'.
In your 'sweet little Alice blue gown',
'But when Irish eyes are smiling'
'Glasgow goes round and round'.

'Amazing Grace' 'What a wonderful world'
'How can you tell me you're lonely'.
That you miss 'the old folks at home',
'Everything is beautiful, in its own way'.
'As time goes by' 'I'll hear you sigh'
So 'I'll take you home again Kathleen'.

'Hello Dolly, it's so nice to see back where you belong'
'You are my sunshine' right or wrong.
'All things bright and beautiful'
'This is my story, this is my song'
'One day at a time, sweet Jesus'
And 'When I fall in love' 'Danny Boy'
'Show me the way to go home'.

'It's a long way to Tipperary', 'Sally, Sally'
'Wish me luck as you wave me goodbye'
'Pack all your troubles in your old kitbag'
And follow me to 'The land of hope and glory'
'There'll be pennies from Heaven' 'Over the rainbow',
'After the ball was over'. 'Bye, bye blackbird'.

Millicent Colwell

SPIDERS IN THE BATH

Why is it in September?
That these pests arrive,
Not only just the wasps,
Looking for somewhere to survive,

Moths and Daddy-long-legs,
They all appear at night,
Both of these two species,
Are attracted to the light,

But what about the spider?
That we find in the bath,
It really is not funny,
There is no need to laugh,

Do they come up through the plughole?
Or through the overflow?
Or drop down from the ceiling?
And don't know where to go,

Have they climbed up the side?
To see what is within,
One thing that is for certain,
They'll have to go before I get in.

Martin J Harvey

MADAME TUSSAUDS

I went to Madame Tussauds,
To see the house of wax.
The statues stood quite lifelike,
I'm never going back.

I went down to the basement,
Each step the lights grew dim,
Dark and cold, blood chilling,
Black walls were closing in.

Hannibal and Dr Crippen,
The Exorcist by the bed,
Car crash on the motorway,
The blood went from my head.

Helping hands did guide me,
To the first stony stair,
I staggered up to brightness,
To feel the seaside air.

I've been to Madame Tussauds
Everything portrayed in wax,
Worth every penny paid
But I'm never going back.

Jean Neville

THE PLEASURES OF AUTUMN

Autumn is a colourful season
The county's a joy to behold.
With trees all ablaze with autumn hues,
And landscape of brown, green and gold.

Red poppies add a splash of colour,
Yellow dandelions dot the verge.
Hedgerows bright berried, as hips and haws
And the fruit of the bramble emerge.

September's the time to start harvesting
Our vegetables, apples and pears.
Time for planting spring bulbs, sowing seeds, tidying up.
Lots of jobs for the gardener who cares.

In October there's Harvest Thanksgiving,
Thanking God for the fruits of the earth.
We see the leaves fall and scatter around
Late blooms hang on, proving their worth.

Our days are now rather changeable -
One day chilly with frosts, next day warm.
The month ends traditionally with the Eve of all Hallows,
When children dress up to perform.

November is the month for protecting and pruning,
Most trees are now bare, but the evergreen grows.
Bonfire night's celebrated with fireworks and feasts,
And Armistice Day reveres our lost war heroes.

The last days of autumn are just lingering on,
But those early bright colours have faded, or gone.

Jocelyn Lander

CHLOE ANN

My sister Chloe Ann was born
Just yesterday before the dawn.
She's rosy-pink and very small,
And has no hair or teeth at all.

She's tiny fingers, curly toes,
And such a funny button nose.
She looks at me with squiffy eyes,
And screws her face up when she cries.

I hoped that she'd come out to play -
I waited all of yesterday,
I waited all this afternoon,
But mummy says it's much too soon.

She cannot walk or talk, you know,
And mummy says she's got to grow,
And says that she is far too small
To throw or catch a rubber ball.

I keep on peeping in the cot -
She doesn't seem to grow a lot!
Each time I go to have a peep
She's snuggled up and fast asleep.

I'm tired of waiting all the day
For little Chloe Ann to play
Until a baby sister's one
A kitten is a lot more fun!

Ann Dempsey

HE IS NOT HERE, 'THE LORD IS RISEN'
(Matt 28v6)

He is not here, 'The Lord is risen'
The tomb is empty now,
For God has raised Him from the dead
Now glory crowns His brow

The rock hewn tomb could never hold
The blessed Christ of God
The fact that he would rise again
Is written in God's word

The cruel crown of piercing thorns
No longer crowns His brow
His hands and feet no longer nailed
Are seen in glory now

Our glorious Lord, raised from the dead
A mighty victor He
Now sits upon His throne above
His victory makes us free.

The King of King and Lords of Lords
Exalted now in Heaven
Adored by all His blood bought church
Who know their sins forgiven

Soon He will come to claim His bride
And her, to glory raise
The church triumphant, now in Heaven
United in His praise

So keep us Lord till that great day
Close to Thy wounded side
Watching and waiting 'Till He come'
Jesus once crucified.

Horace Hartley

CHOICE

You created me in a specific way,
Moulded me from underground clay.
You set me down, upon the earth,
With emotions ranging from
Sadness to mirth.

You knew me, in my mother's womb,
Will recognise me even in the tomb.
If I learn to believe your word,
Act upon what you did, what I've heard.

Your words are like food to me,
Without you Dear Jesus
Where would I be?
For this world would attempt to
Convince me it's wrong.
Relying on the Bible, so true and strong.

I know that you love me Lord
I need to live by
Your two-edged sword.
I choose to drink the living water
And remain for eternity
Your faithful daughter.

I'll remember my God what you did
So I could choose to be a *Kingdom Kid.*

Lousie White

A-RHYMING GO WE

Parsley, sage, rosemary and thyme
A rhyme is a rhyme is a rhyme.

But rhyming is so stuffy, it's for old fuddy-duddies.
Now, just look at young trendies,
The way their verse flows, unbroken by
The stumbling-block of rhyme - aye,
But removing a major difficulty
Is hardly a proof of superiority.

Very well, but rhyming is bourgeois, it's for the ruling-class.
Haven't you read folk ballads, Blake, Burns? You little ass,
The People's Poetry
Dwells woven into a rich rhyming tapestry.

Cudgelling one's brains, burning the midnight oil,
Rhyme-hunting is hard toil.
Pursuing the elusive note that will complete the harmony
Is to dedication a loving testimony.

So 'Go fetch me a pint o' wine'
And, any time,
Gladden my heart with an honest rhyme,
Parsley, sage, rosemary and thyme.

Jackie S Brent

THE CONFESSION

Dear Father, I have a confession to make,
My standard of living may well be at stake.
My life is not lustful, evil or frolic,
My confession is this: I'm a chocoholic.

When I started college they made me do astrology,
But all it did was show me the delights of gastroenterology.
The stars simply weren't that interesting and so throughout the day,
I'd sit alone and eat the entire Milky Way.

Then, at the canteen, my eyes met his across the floor.
This was it! The real thing! True love! I was sure.
He came over and offered me his final chocolate orange segment.
Three months later I did a test and found out I was pregnant.

He said that he'd stand by me. He said he'd always be there,
That we'd be fused together, that we'd be two of a pair.
He ran off with my best friend - all he'd said was fallacy.
He left me roses, a dear-John note and a dim view of the galaxy.

So I had the kid Father, but our estate's beset by crime,
And it wasn't long before they'd stolen our last dime.
My life is all in pieces and I'm only a young girl,
But each day I feel I'm sliding down a giant hazelnut whirl.

I went to the Council. They made it all seem clear.
They promised to get me a flat, you know, something not too dear,
Somewhere I'd feel safe with more bobbies on the beat,
So I ended up residing at 4a Quality Street.

So here I am Father, here to ask for absolution,
Hoping that your prayers will grant me a solution,
That through the intercession of Matthew, Luke and Peter,
I'll be able to get through tomorrow - the fateful day of Easter.

Lisa Parry

THE BEACH

I look out at the mountains surrounded by the sea
The waves come rolling past me and I wonder where they have been.
The boats are bobbing gently in the breeze along the shore
As I laze on the beach my mind wanders on dreams and more.

The sun beats down upon me, its heat too hot to take
I shrink beneath the umbrella, and wonder when I'll bake.
I don't really like it, but you have got to get a tan
I'll persevere gently with the oil and sun spray can.

My book lies idly by me as I gaze across the bay
The gentle lapping of the waves sends my reading mood away
The sea looks enticing as the sun reaches its peak,
I put my feet on the blazing sand, and cringe against its heat.

Do I really want to go into that cool and distant sea?
Scramble among the umbrellas, chairs and families.
Sun seekers lie everywhere, spread-eagled on the sand
The water's cool and soothing, but I seem a long way from the land.

I look out at the mountains surrounded by the sea
The waves come rolling past me and I wonder where they have been.
I start to wade towards the shore, which seems so far away
I feel good, and so relaxed, it's been a fantastic holiday.

Sheila M Storr

PROCREATION

All animals seek a mate
It is in our genes to procreate
Whether male or female the urge is there
It is nature in the raw, stripped bare

Our genes ensure it is our strongest instinct
It is the necessity for all species to keep their line distinct
By ensuring there is a next generation existing and strong
And evolution theory suggests that new favourable traits are
also carried along

It seems incredible but it could well be right
That over the course of countless millennia of day and night
All living creatures by this method reach their present perfection
And as the environment changes they respond and themselves
also change by continuing their procreation

What a source of unbelievable wonder all living creatures are!
The poet Coleridge's Ancient Mariner becalmed and alone
initially did slimy sea fish bar
Until God took pity on him and made him look again
Forgiving his Albatross killing and his dreadful character stain

He then did see anew and spellbound the fishes rich attire
With their every movement tracing our flashes of golden fire
'O happy living things!' unwittingly he cried
And a prayer of love for all life welled up enveloping him inside

The Albatross straightway fell from his neck
And the dead motionless corpses stirred upon the deck
As the ship now expertly navigated by an unknown hand
Took back to port the Ancient Mariner and his ship's ghostly band

Is there a message here for us to heed in procreation?
We surely delude ourselves that we are masters of all creation
As flora and fauna worldwide by us are wantonly destroyed
Leading to an inevitable ending of Man alone and living in a void

Yes, the alternative as I see it as God's way is instead to see all other life as not unworthy but as creatures as beautiful and wonderful as are we ourselves

And moreover just as worthy of living and procreation instead of being killed off and seen only as extinct life exhibited on dusty museum shelves.

Frank Hansford-Miller

AMERICA, WITH YOU WE MOURN
(September 11, 2001)

America with you we mourn,
But is the terror at an end,
Or has the world a new black dawn?
For countries each on each depend.

Wherever next may terror strike?
- Wherever next may chaos be?
From murderous and mad dislike
Will we again such pictures see?

America, we too are sad
For our own dead we also mourn
Since evil forces have gone mad,
We too have grieving folks forlorn.

Frances Joan Tucker

A RHYME IN TIME

Now English is a funny tongue,
It trips up linguists old and young,
The hair they tear out's turning grey,
For what you see ain't what you say.

You'd think that 'though' would rhyme with 'through'
And that, my friend, is the first of the few . . .
Yes, few *thousand* that confound the crowd -
But thinking aloud is not allowed.

Is there another language where
The exception proves the rule? Don't care!
A masochist, I love this language,
Exciting as a Danish sandwich.

So, keep your PC spell-check dear,
It can't distinguish 'hear' from 'here'.
This glorious tongue, so versatile,
Requires humour, strength and guile!

D M Anderson

DOWN MEMORY LANE

I took a stroll down memory lane,
And there I saw it all so plain,
The village green beside the burn,
And far above the hill of Durn.

The fun, the laughter, the childish game,
So long ago, 'tis not the same,
A ghostly silence lingers through,
Where once each single one I knew.

The gypsies camping sometimes where
A circus was held in 'Hallowfair',
The Blacksmith, Tailors, the Village Store,
Alas to say they are no more,
But in my memories there they'll stay,
Reminiscence of another day.

Annie McKimmie

EVERLASTING LOVE

My love for you is everlasting
It rules each day and night
And I am so unhappy
When you are out of sight
There are tears in my eyes
And pain in my heart
The days are all so lonely
Whilst we are apart
Missing you so much my darling
I wish that you could see
My life would be so happy
If you came home to me.

Diana Daley

FLAKES

From the long study window a falling of snow
Snow was now gently falling upon fallen snow
Winter has finally come - now we know

To build a snowman out of the deep snow
Leaves your mittens damp and fingers aglow
On frosty nights when icy winds blow upon blow
Snuggle up to the fire against the lamp glow

On dry crisp nights - see heaven's star show
But come the spring - we'll have melting snow
Races down mountains - flow upon flow
Until the winter winds again begin to blow

David Charles

MORNING MIST

From what fairy land have you quietly come,
Ghostly, insubstantial mist?
Hovering over fields, wrapped in your tears,
Wreathing among trees that you softly kiss.
As you gently lie over hill and vale
We see our land in a softer vein.
Contours soften where you lie
But time has come for you to die.
Your life is short, you cannot stay
In wisps of grey you fade away.
Silent you came, as silently go,
Wraith-like disappearing in morning's glow.

Margaret Renshaw

IN SEPTEMBER

Heat of summer mellows
Into autumn's gentler sun;
Mists of morning show a kindlier light.
Flowers, in their glory
Till their last display is done,
Cheer our hearts and fill us with delight.

Nature's bounty beckons
From the fields and from the trees;
Ripened berries shine among the leaves.
Apples glow from treetops,
Branches tossing in the breeze;
Standing corn the final cut receives.

Now the swallows gather
On the wires, prepared for flight,
Soon their epic journey will begin
Into summer country,
Where the sun will still be bright,
Leaving winter to their hardier kin.

As the leaves are turning
To their brave autumnal shades,
Racing clouds are driven by the winds,
On towards the year's end,
When the gaudy colour fades
And the winter resting time begins.

Joy Jenkins

YOGA'S THE THING!

The *first* thing about yoga is to breathe
As your limbs into contortions start to weave
Just inhale slowly and prepare
To fill your lungs with good fresh air
You'll be feeling more relaxed before you leave!

The *next* thing about yoga is to pose
Lying on your front or standing on your toes
Tie your body's every cranny
In a reef knot or a granny
Then just exhale - and touch the floor with your nose!

But the *last* thing about yoga is the *best*
Put your yogic meditation to the test
Stop the stretching and the straining
Make your body stop complaining
Just get comfy - clear your mind - and take a rest!

Chris Waddington

AFTERSHOCK

The cruel earth contorts with fearsome force;
The heaving rock destroys my dear home town
And as I sleep my world turns upside down.
Worst fears come true as bedlam takes its course.

I can't shut out the screams, the stench, the pain,
The heat, the dust, the darkness, God - the thirst!
With shouts for help my lungs begin to burst
And nightmares terrorise my tortured brain.

Where is my baby? Where's my wife, oh, where?
I claw at rubble; panic fuels my fear.
The rescuers move on. They've left me here.
My gleam of hope becomes a dark despair.

My home - my warm, my safe protective womb -
In seconds turned into my hellish tomb.

Keith Ellel

STEP INSIDE

Step inside the door,
One can only step in awe;
Of what men built
Centuries before.
Hand cut to size,
Perfect stone arches,
Broad and wide.
Upwards too glass roof domes.
Leaded light;
Reflect on leaded engrave;
Foot worn, paving stone floors,
Chiselled oak wooden flowers; scene
Decorate partitions floral screens.
Rich and poor,
The church roof,
Needs a restore.
An ask can not be ignored.
For money a plea,
One heard before,
Same charity blow
Centuries old.
To collect money,
To plug the same old roof holes
For centuries, the roof
Needs a restore.

B G Clarke

THE COLOUR BROWN

Of all the colours amazing everyone,
Seascapes, green glorious, emblazoned with sun,
The celestial blue of canopied skies,
Why is it all brown shade I choose to disguise?

Brown, deep and chocolate, stirs love in dog's eyes,
Mahogany chestnuts roll out in surprise,
Sheraton furniture, log fires burnish brown,
And amber, autumnal leaves magic down.

So why not give purple and scarlet a break,
Different tones entirely colour schemes make,
Soft, velvety sepia lashes on peach,
On the cheeks of little brown children I teach?

Brown is miraculous, as usable as cream,
It penetrates boredom, inhabits my dream,
Forget not the merman's russet mane,
And those of dear horses, contriving again,
To flaunt racing browness despite of their pain.

Ruth Daviat

NINE MINUTES

I am sitting at the table,
Completely out of stamps
My typewriter isn't working,
That's 'cause I have the cramps,
The envelopes are all used up,
My pen is out of ink,
I am feeling very thirsty,
With not a drop to drink.

I called to see you last week,
Also the week before,
I could not find the doorbell,
So I hammered on the door,
I was going to try again today,
But my car is out of fuel,
So I thought that I would phone you,
But hadn't paid the bill.

There was only one thing I could do;
'Twas to have a walk around,
But I found my shoes had holes in,
So my feet are on the ground,
My bike tyres have no air in,
So I stay to take a bath, no hope!
'Cause the water heater's broken,
And I am out of soap.

I am sure you must be fed up,
With all my tales of woe,
But I thought that I would sit down,
And have a little go,
To see how long it would take,
This took me just nine minutes,
Don't know if you could beat that,
But it's not too bad now . . . init?

J Deekes

FEARFUL TERROR

Fearful terror come from the sky
Out of the blue, 'danger' shouts cry
Fire storm, dust, metal, concrete falls
Skyscraper shudder, frantic calls
Last words from those about to die

Senseless slaughter as we ask why
Waste of life, souls we cannot buy
Dust and ash, where towers stood tall
Fearful terror

Just another regular guy
Who could know to their deaths they fly?
Nameless engulfed in fireball
From glass and rock, survivors crawl
Resurrection; dead wait - still, lie;
Fearful terror . . .

Megan ÒCriogàin

TRIP TO MARS

He there, I'm Jack,
Pleased to see you,
I've just come back
From foreign places far and wide
I've even been to the other side
To see the Martians upon Mars
It's really nice amongst the stars
Travelling first class to Jupiter and Mars
But silly me fell down the stairs
And everyone just stood and stared
Not one of them did seem to care
And in my dreams I heard them say
Welcome aboard our Apollo Eight
The strangest music did they play
So relaxing I wanted to stay.
The strangest food I got to taste
But it smelt so bad it went to waste
It really belonged on a refuse cart
And was so bad it made me fart
Which got us all off to a bad start
Not a nice way to win a heart
Or get to know the man from Mars.

Sue Peach

MEMORIES

Open the book of memories in your mind,
Turn the pages carefully and there you'll find,
Everyone has been stored and pressed,
To you pick the one that you like the best,
Good friends and happy days gone by,
Where you've laughed so much you could cry,
Christmas and birthdays too,
Memories of special friends like you,
And though there's times yet to come,
Your book of memories will store each one.

A P Starling

REMEMBERING

As lorries and cars go hurtling by
Causing pollution to rise to the sky
I remember the days of long ago
When the pace of life was gentle and slow.

Each day I'd walk the country lane
Between fields of swaying golden grain.
I'd climb to the top of the rocky ridge
Then rest coming down by the old stone bridge.

I would listen to the countryside sounds
While watching the dragonflies hover around.
A splash in the river as salmon leap
Disturbed baby ducks from their afternoon sleep.

But now that lane has disappeared.
Unfortunately never to reappear.
The fields of grain are now a parking lot.
The old stone bridge became a picnic spot.

That quiet lane I walked each day
Is now concrete called a motorway.
No hidden bends or gentle curves.
No beauty for me to observe.

Just streams of traffic hurtling by
Polluting the landscape and the sky.
Oh for those days of long ago
When the pace of life was gentle and slow.

Sue Davan

A Rhyming Challenge

A challenge is a rhyme
  Inside time, p'rhaps outside time?
T'speak of the sublime . . .
  T'remain silent, would be, a crime
Would it not?
  For, what have (we) got
That we ain't been given?

The *Lord*, is the Lord of this rhyme;
  Inside of time, He died: outside time
He now reigns . . . the sublime:
  T'ignore Him, would be, the crime
Would it not?
  If we do . . . we may rot!
His blood's been shed: He's forgiven,

(Thru faith in Him) those that believe,
  And thru His Spirit comes relief
For those on their spiritual knees . . .
  P'rhaps (they) in this world don't succeed!
What's 'that' mean, you say!
  Well: who needs succour? For whom do yer pray
But they, that ain't got what you've got?

And what have yer got? Well, a lot!
  For once 'pon a time, I was not
Aware that the King gave (me) my lot:
  At that time, of our God, I was 'shot',
But, He never got 'shot' of me!
  And now, thru faith in Him - I'm free
To live with Him - for eternity . . .

A challenge is a rhyme . . .
  Thru Christ we're offered
                    The sublime!

Anon

ARISTOCAT

Silk or satin cushions,
Well-upholstered chairs,
Cosy beds with eiderdowns
Are what Puss most prefers.
After the dainty concoctions
Her master chef prepares,
After her ablutions,
She softly climbs the stairs.

While unfortunate poor relations,
Slinky, wild alley cats
Out in all weather conditions
Hunt for mice and rats,
Fighting for recognition
From the local female cats,
Declaring their admiration
In ecstatic sharps and flats.

Hard life! But what elation!
What courage! What hard graft!
Though they've had tribulation
At least they've fully lived.
If our Puss had their station
She'd die - she's much too soft.
She's just a decoration
And might as well be stuffed!

I love my comforts and my ease.
From rigorous life I shrink,
But though hard things me never please
They're good for me, I think.
So, Lord, still daily for me choose,
Draw me back from this brink.
Teach me to love you more than these,
Lest I in softness sink.

V M Archer

DEVIL HOLD ME TIGHT

Deep in my head
Lies a dream I am dead.
And I see your eyes,
Dark and round.
And your lips
Make no sound.
Devil hold me tight.

Fear seems to flood.
I feel my skin dressed in mud.
And I see your eyes,
Dark and round.
And feel my arms,
Tightly bound.
Devil hold me tight.

Cold is my grave.
Now I know I'm death's slave.
And I see your eyes,
Dark and cold.
And your face
Looks so old.
Devil hold me tight.

Peter Steele

BROTHER

I had a brother
good looking and strong
oh my brother
where did it go wrong.

Strong and opinionated
has to have his say
I'm sorry my brother
I'm not the type to obey.

I have my family
a life and friends
do you want *our* relationship
to end?

Anyone else
I couldn't give a toss
do you want us
to get lost?

Passing in the street
looking the other way
come on Gordon
what do you say?

When you get to my age
you can't live in a rage
you can't take life too serious
let's start a fresh new page.

It's up to you my brother
I am all you've got
don't kick me in the face, my brother
even though I'm the one you fought.

Jacqueline Dunn

TEARS, ON THE DEATH OF MY HUSBAND

I've seen some tears in my lifetime, I've watched them rise and fall
The tears that I'm now shedding are the bitterest of them all,
I've carefully dried the others yet mine I cannot dry,
They're deep within my very soul, yes! in my very sigh,
They're the tears of no explaining, they leave lines upon my face,
I guess that all I'm suffering must leave its silent trace.

Jean A Smith

PAPER AND PEN

They say the pen is mightier than the sword,
As the outcome is greater by the written word,
A whole world opens with the things that you write,
For someone to praise them is a sheer delight,
Your mind is expanded with the knowledge you acquire,
When you edit your words in the way you desire,
If your mind is kept active the goals you achieve,
Can outweigh your problems and set you at ease,
So, with positive thinking you will achieve your goal,
But never for one moment think that you are too old.

Alan Fordham

ETHNIC CLEANSE

The veneer of civilisation is a very thin line.
Is this why we see it time after time
as, within a community, the veneer stars to tear
exposing the evil that's there,
as the civilised spirit of neighbours and friends
is torn wide apart, to become 'ethnic cleanse'?
How does it happen? How does it start?
How is a neighbourhood torn wide apart?
How does hysteria become the rule
making people vindictive and so terribly cruel,
abusing and maiming those once known as friends,
all in the name of 'ethnic cleanse'?

Alison Birket

PARALLELS

Sun, moon; dull, bright,
Sky, sea; depth, height.
Old, new; clean, worn,
Start, end; die, born.
Feel, hear; loud, touch,
Large, small; little, much.
Seek, have; want, find,
Love, hate; cruel, kind.
Through, round; by, in,
Hope, wish; lose, win.

I D Coxall

DOUBLE DUTCH DITTY

A poem that rhymes, now what shall I rhyme?
A ditty for children to skip
I'll rhyme for a time, it will not be a crime
If you'll twined your rope and not trip.

If you'll not scab your knee, I will rhyme, one, two, three
That's it, jump dear, jump, dear jump
The rhythm I chant, I'll call it you see
Shoulders back, children, posture, don't slump.

Two ropes? Oh dear, now isn't that clever
Careful, be careful, oh my
Shirley you've been, I think it's now Trevor
Well of course you can't, if you don't try.

Me have a go? Oh I don't think so. No!
It wouldn't be fitting for Miss.
Am I doing it now? Oh, please do go slow.
I'm getting the hang now of this.

Don't go faster, this isn't such fun
I'm getting myself in a twist.
See, look what you've done, I'm down on my bum
And I've broken my ankle and wrist.

Sue Simpson

AUTUMN

Grey, grim and grandiose,
the sharp frostbite that nips the nose:
To follow stifling heat that cloys
comes Autumn with its charm and joys.

Crisp and dry beneath my foot,
the leaves of trees that won't stay put.
A time to be and stay indoors,
or walk the golden outward floors.

Alive and free:
Vital, vibrant artistry;
the passions and desires I know
through quickened veins now freely flow.

The magic waft of season's mist
imparts a welcome, solemn kiss;
to kindle former memories,
awaken me to hopes and dreams.

Wistful willows, prime prowess.
Sleeping bloom, ripe fullness.
The stirring of the inner sense
and epitome of soul's incense.

Caroline Baker

PROCRASTINATION

Don't leave it too late, they said, come soon,
Your cottage is waiting beside the lake;
The new green is springing among the brake;
And in copses the bluebells start to wake;
In thickets the courting ring-doves croon -
Don't leave it too late, come soon!

So we talked it over, the wife and I,
Reviewed our resources and balance books
With pencil and paper and long hard looks;
Unmindful of gardens and inglenooks,
Unheeding the call of a lark on high
Far off in a summer sky.

We counted the cost of all our needs
And the sum was always beyond our score,
So we went on working just as before
While the cottage stood empty upon the shore,
And a sad wind whispered among the reeds
And the garden grew over with weeds.

But now the grass is again new-mown,
And standing at eve at the cottage gate
I ponder the truth of the words 'too late',
For the step that my ears once used to await
Has followed the lark to a height unknown,
And I stand in the dusk alone.

R Probert

A SHOT IN THE ARM

Nothing inspires me,
Nothing can shock.
I have a condition
They call 'writer's block'.

Lethargy traps me
Here in my room.
Outside is sunshine,
Inside is gloom.

Even the postman
Brings only bills;
No billets doux,
Nothing that thrills.

The letterbox rattles,
My heart gives a jump
When down on the mat
An envelope thumps.

Inspiration is soaring,
My spirits revive
For 'Poetry Now'
Has once more arrived.

Helen Strangwige

LIFE

What tender thread life hangs upon,
One day here, laughing, loving, hating,
The next day gone.

What precious time is wasted when
We spend it wishing, grumbling, envying
Our fellow men.

In youth we seem to set the pace
So fast, for our exciting, busy, restless
Human race.

But with maturity, reflections seem
To hold us in a reminiscent, clouded
World of dreams.

With loved ones gone, some without warning,
We're left to grieve, give thanks for life,
Yet wonder for the morning . . .

Joan Hammond

MITCH

Silver and grey was his coat.
A beautiful head; the greenest of eyes
burst through the Venetian blinds.
This cat literally fell into our lives.

On a small farm of fruit trees
Mitch cast his spell over all.
Was escort to the farm dairy,
ensured the snappy dog's fall.

Nor did the cobra phase him.
Mitch stopped further advance.
The cobra, hesitant, turned to retire,
not staking life to chance.

Aboard ship in care of the lamp trimmer
Mitch had a ball.
A berth on his bed, star of the fancy dress
Dick Whittington's cat was known to all.

Robert Allen

SEASONS

Spring has come the birds are singing,
Hear the distant church bells ringing.
Listen to the choirs singing,
Happiness fills the air.

Summer's here, the larks on high
Flying through the cloudless sky.
Meadows green where cattle lie,
Laughter's in the air.

Mellow autumn's here again,
Harvests safely gathered in.
Dew hangs low in the shady glen.
Bonfires scent the air.

See the winter clothed in white,
Jack Frost sparkles in the night.
Hear the bells on the special night.
Magic in the air.

E Timmins

THE SILENCER

Hush, now, hush, the iceman's coming,
See his shadow, feel his breath.
Stalactites encrust the plumbing,
Crystallise in sudden death.
Close your eyes, his hand is near you,
Hearken to the drum he plays,
Bearing evergreens to spear you,
Crucifixion of your days.
Comes with paralysing ice
To dump the carcass on the cart,
Whispering: it is the price
For overburdening the heart.
He stops, then shuffles on his way.
Sleep, now, sleep, at close of day.

Faith Bissett

EVERY MOMENT IS LOVE

Like dreams blessed by heaven
Like words in a prayer
My faith is eternal
With the moments I share
I'm born with a promise
In a heavenly light
And fate is my teacher
Passing the secrets of life
As does every dawn flower
To live in my eyes
Every day brings me nearer
To my ultimate prize
As does every spring blossom
Love came for my soul
And entered my being
Letting a prophecy unfold
This was always my destiny
That was dreamt up above
A place in your heart
Where every moment is love

David Bridgewater

FIGHT THE GOOD FIGHT

'Fight the good fight', a prayer and then he starts
His rambling sermon, theme - 'Lift up your hearts'.
Hymn, benediction, time to grab a crust,
Hospice-bound, the old Ford kicks the dust.

Sleeping? Peace is hers seen through the slit
In curtain folds around the bed. What wit
She shows where pain is so immense,
'Dear father, there's no feeling, there's no sense!'

She is the apple of her father's eye, and more,
He will not see her as a browning core.
She loves him, man of God and high esteem,
He prays for mercy and for hope - there is a gleam.

Fight the good fight as chemotherapy strikes
At all deep-seated cankers and their likes.

Geoff Dickes

MAIDEN AUNT EDITH

My mother's youngest sister was clever, tall and kind,
You'd think amongst her suitors a special one she'd find.
No doubt a number asked her, but never 'Yes' she'd say
As long as the marriage service contained that word 'obey'.

She had to earn her living, for her parson-father died
While she was still at boarding school; her elder sisters tried
But 'governess' or 'companion' was all that they could find;
'Jane Eyre' was still the pattern for 'young ladies' of their kind.

But for Edith in the Nineties, the choice was getting wider;
A clerkship in the Post Office would a living wage provide her.
Behind the scenes, in privacy, but never out on show
'Accounts' employed 'young ladies' - she was fortunate, I know.

But promises were promises, not lightly undertaken -
Aunt Edith told the tale herself if I am not mistaken -
She wasn't going to say 'obey' to any man or boy,
So all her life my maiden aunt her freedom could enjoy.

Ahead of time, this lively girl to business was devoted,
Her colleagues all took umbrage when Aunt Edith was promoted.
Some forty girls beneath her, so I heard my Auntie say -
Were they jealous, now I wonder, of 'the one that got away'?

Kathleen M Hatton

BELIEVING

The hardest thing in life to bear
Is to want someone who isn't there
But when you see a star shine through
You know that person's there with you
Locked away inside your heart
Forever there when you're feeling blue.

There beside you through thick and thin
If you should need them, look within
For love can never split in two
It's inside them, it's inside you
Love can never tear apart
It remains forever within our hearts.

Maria Jenkinson

NIGHTFALL

Across the lane a gardener prunes his roses,
And the rushing cars throb quickly along the road below,
The blackbird sings undaunted in the early evening chill,
And rooftops gleam redly in the fading sunset glow,
Here are curtained windows keeping out enfeebled light,
Dimming rooms where sleeping children quietly lie,
Distant hills and moors are still and purpling darkly,
And frogs in the valley listen to the river as it rushes by,
In a field a horse is moving quietly in the shadows,
His ambling footsteps soundless on the deep and growing grass,
Two lovers stroll along the footpath holding hands and dreaming,
But the horse is all unknowing, not even glancing as they pass,
The last few feathered creatures sing their sweet nocturne,
And lights begin to shine in windows, one by one,
With respite from toil, a welcome healing seems to form,
When quiet peace proclaims that day is done,
Almost sighing, the once-busy day departs gently,
People enter homes and leave the fading scene,
The fine day has given golden satisfaction,
And now the evening breeze blows cool and clean,
In their homes the people gather secretly, lock their doors and hide,
The velvety darkness now enfolds them keeping them from sight,
And then, except from afar, no creature stirs, no sound disturbs,
And the world slumbers through the silent night.

Win Wilcock

TANG WHESSER

He was only a young pup seal
barely encountered his first square meal
the realisation soon sunk in, he was not alone
he had arrived in a kindergarten, gene-pool seal sanctuary zone

In the greater plan of things he was alone
as the playful days were not to last
and he soon came to learn that bullets were fast
for maybe his chances were slim
that big hairy man in the boat wanted his skin.

John M Heddle

MAGICAL MYSTERY TOUR

A day on a magical mystery tour
so many things to explore
a castle, a church, or tavern or much more.

Steps that are far too steep my eyes do peek
romantic shores or a picnic by the river
such dazzling scenery for a beginner

Strawberry teas or a cricket match or three
forest trees that are deeply dark
to children that this game is a lark

Watching sheep on fields that are green
to blackberry picking,
the juiciest fruits you have ever seen

Windmills turning their heads
to lighthouse, shining
it's time for bed

Well it's time for the bus
homebound if we must.

A J Renyard

THE CROW

A crow flew up as I approached,
And flapped a grudging circle round.
Then as I passed, no more encroached,
It swooped and settled on the ground.

Its one objective, smeared and red,
Lay pinioned 'neath its grasping feet.
It pulled, and ripped at flesh now dead
And risked the road its fill to eat.

Next day, that way I chose to go,
And sped across the mist-kissed heath.
A night and morn of carnage so
Abysmal caked the road beneath.

And there ahead, atop a crest,
Edged in on left and right by trees,
A listless sail waved east then west,
Caught on the morning's gentle breeze.

The sail slipped down as zephyrs failed,
And sadly slid beneath my car,
Was now in black and red regaled,
And never more would fly afar.

Alan Day

SUMMERTIME

All around looks so beautiful
On a warm summer's day,
With fields of corn now golden
And the fragrance of fresh mown hay,
All nature suddenly comes alive
The bees are busy in their hives,
Trees adorned in shades of green
A babbling brook clear and clean,
Birds flittering from here and there
Or soaring high into the air,
The sky above of palest blue
Maybe a wisp of cloud of two,
At sunset a ball of fire
A beautiful scene one has to admire,
The red glow left once the sun has gone
Later turns to a mottled sky
As the evening wears on
A cool breeze fans the heat of the day
As night clouds gather I silently pray,
Thanks to God for a perfect day.

O Godfrey

MOMENTS TO REMEMBER

I lie awake and say a prayer,
Knowing in my heart that you're not there.
But as the darkness takes the light,
Still in my mind you're burning bright.
To think of all the joys we shared,
And how we always loved and cared,
I give my thanks for times we had,
And looking back was not so bad.
So dear the memory of those hours,
Where every pathway led to flowers,
And with a full heart's thankful sighs,
Remember the bliss before my eyes.

Elisabeth Dill Perrin

OUR EDEN

It was dusk-light and the ending
Of the party we had been;
And its music still about us
Our partners held between.

We left old tubby London
A-wheezing in the dawn,
With its blight of crippled pigeons
Eating pasta on the lawn.

While the car in which we travelled
At a speed of rash content,
With its crew of blissful pilgrims,
Turned southward down to Kent,

Where we reached a sleepy orchard
With tight curls of teeming fruit
And our mouths so smoothly empty
From the bottles in the boot.

That we spread our shirts and filled 'em
With armfuls of 'moons',
Till the branches sprung upwards
Like deflated balloons.

And the many round faces
We'd shook from out the sprays
Took on reflection of our own
That we bit into for days.

Then oh, but how we sparkled,
And never knew a care,
In that early world of Adamite
And appled air . . .

We were young . . . and we were happy
Like notes of purest pan,
That crackled in the cornlight
Before the world began.

Derrick Porter

TO MY VALENTINE

Oh won't you be my valentine?
You know my heart is truly thine;
I go all weak and start to pine
When I see you on the Central Line.
Your countenance is so benign,
It's hard to believe you're sixty-nine -
It's true your teeth no longer shine
And you look like Michael Hestletine -
But I'd follow you from the source of the Rhine
To the crumbling cliffs of Blackgang Chine.
Come, walk with me in the pale moonshine
And weave my hair with eglantine,
And then the two of us shall dine
On caviar, oysters and red wine.
Just serenade me with a line
From that lovers' lilt 'Fog On The Tyne'
Or 'Oh My Darling Clementine',
Either of those would be just fine.
And then, at last, our hearts will entwine
Like Harlequin and Columbine.
Oh please, my love, give me a sign
To say that soon you will be mine.
What's that? You feel you must decline
My offer? What a bloody swine!
I always thought you looked bovine -
Well, s** off then, you philistine!

Julia May Martin

58

RHYME

Some say that a poem should rhyme,
That last words should match up every time,
But words are elusive,
My brain's like a sieve,
So I'd much rather write in blank verse.

Great poets have mastered the art,
Their verses come straight from the heart,
With passionate love song
Their feelings give tongue,
As they pour out their feelings in verse.

Some write of events of great note,
On victorious battles they dote,
They describe every shot
And manoeuvre, the lot,
An epic narration in verse.

Famed Shakespeare and Wordsworth wrote odes,
But they could have been written in codes
For I cannot do it,
My words do not fit,
I can't get the hang of this verse!

In dreams I can rhyme every line
And finding the words is just fine,
They come into my head
As I lie there in bed,
I'm an absolute genius in verse!

But when I awake it's no go,
Not one single rhyme do I know,
So I'll give up the fight
And I'll only write
The much easier lines of blank verse!

Roma Davies

SPRING

The spring is the start of a new beginning.
When trees and flowers show signs of living.
The bare and cold unfriendly earth
Makes a start to show its worth,
By bringing forth growth in splendid colour
Which lifts my heart, and many another.
The yellow daffodils sway in the breeze.
The little blue crocuses vie with these,
The birds bring their fledglings to perch on my wall
While others saucily fly down to call.
How far this seems from the maddening crowd,
With cars rushing by and the noise so loud.
The music blares, how the decibels rise,
I go indoors, and subdue my sighs.

Kathleen Holmes

THE DESERT SCENE

All day the sun had blazed
upon the sterile land.
The sculptured hills and ridges
lay cast of golden sand.
No clouds to drift along the sky,
even the wind had died.
The haze ascended wraith-like,
the sky to earth was tied.

The sharp-edged hills climb
as high to touch the sun.
The smooth, silk slopes sweep
majestically to run.
No rock to cast a shadow,
no creature to be seen,
pray God for rain, for life,
to change the land to green.

Terry Daley

ME AND YOU

The dawning of a new day
Comes around so fast
Eluding moments sprouting
New shoots to form at last
The dying of the old
Making way for all the new
Perhaps that will be the same as well
For both me and you.

A E Jones

TRUE FRIENDS

What are true friends?
They are when the world's at the end
When you're sad
They're beside you when you're glad
To reach out a helping hand
Give all they can
Share all your feelings
All your dealings

Help one another
To make your life fuller
Know your moods
Help if they could
Give a listening ear
To troubles and fear
Lift your spirits high
When you felt you were going to die
Give you all the love you need
Always doing a kind deed
Friends are there to share and care
Make things brighter
Lift your heart lighter
A true friend
Stands by you to the end.

Martin Coyles

LOVE AFFAIR

I opened the window, inviting him in,
Poor little robin, so cold and so thin.
Small bright eyes looked me up, and then down,
Then his feathers fluffed up, like a soft eiderdown.

From the crumbs I gave him he soon took his fill -
Then he was gone from the windowsill.
On cold frosty mornings I gave him a call,
Then he fluttered his wings as he sat on the wall.

His little red waistcoat stood out in the snow,
In the dim morning light as he flew to and fro.
Day after day in the weeks ahead,
He always came for his daily bread.

Then one sad day my heart stood still -
No robin came on the window sill.
I felt that I had lost a friend,
Our love affair was at an end.

In those few weeks he had grown so tame,
Somehow the days were not the same -
Each day that passed seemed cold and grim.
I thought I'd seen the last of him.

Come spring I couldn't believe my eyes!
Two robins came of a different size.
This time he looked at her not me,
He was so proud of her you see.

A tiny bird flew through the door,
And as I picked it up, I saw
A baby robin, soft and warm,
But he was looking all forlorn.

So I talked to him with a gentle sound,
Then placed him where he could be found.

Milly Hatcher

COLD TURKEY

Today's the day zero hour
I am going to stop, I do have the power
Zero + 1 and all my will power has gone
And I'm thinking maybe if I just have one
No I can't, I must last longer
God the craving is getting stronger
God I need a nicotine fix
Just one puff on a cancer stick
I don't know how much more of this I can take
Giving up was definitely a mistake
By six o'clock I'm all tucked up in bed
With ciggies swimming all round my head
Two hours later and I'm still awake
Cos every time I close my eyes
Little lit up ciggies go dancing by
But tomorrow is another day
And I can only hope and pray
That by then the craving has gone away

Philip Robertson

Us

Observing the descending flakes I see
In cool spread water my reflection staring at me
The ripples swim out leaving a blur
Was that someone? Was it her?
I turned around, in a flash she had fled
Rustling leaves swirled around instead
Had my imagination got the better of me?
Slowly my gaze travelled up a tree
Rustling of leaves, the drop of an apple - ever so slight
She may be there - she just might
Scrambling up I graze my hand
Glistening blood trickles on the sand
Taking a twig I write my confession
'I love you' the red a definite impression
Slowly she slips down and touches my hand
Wraps it ever so carefully with her hair band
Hand in hand we walked back slowly
She smiled meaning, she had forgiven me.

Shahmima Khanom

LOVE?

'Do you? Do you?' asked the dove
'Is it me that you love?
Are you sure - are you really?
Do you love me - truly - dearly?
Tell me! Tell me!' said the bird
But the ginger tom just purred!

Lynne Done

THE ANCIENT OCEAN

Long have the crested waves rolled up,
The golden beach to meet,
Long have the foaming shallows washed
Each generation's feet.

Long have the rocks stood tall and proud,
The waters to defy,
Long have the chalky cliffs pushed up
Against the stormy sky.

Long have the wailing seagulls called,
Lost souls across the waste,
Long has the sea thrown up its pearls
In oyster shells encased.

Long has the wind moaned round the rocks
And sighed its mournful sigh,
Long have the waves before me been,
Long after when I die.

Rebecca Nichol

ODE TO A PET HAMSTER

Hammy now has gone to rest,
She's lived her life and left her nest.
We won't be seeing her anymore
Scurrying across the floor
Or spinning round inside her wheel
Working off her latest meal.
We don't know why she breathed her last
But simply mourn a life that's passed
With thanks for all the fun she brought
And know it wasn't all for nought.

David Varley

DOUBLE CHINS

Double chins, treble chins, like galleons in full sail
Setting forth in triumph, we neither shrink nor quail.
Bosoms thrust, heads held high, we know she who dares wins;
Proclaiming a profusion of splendid double chins.

Monserat Caballe, to name but forty-three
Is just the kind of armful everybody likes to see.
When she hits that top note we know it all begins
To vibrate from a larynx encased in double chins.

Let the beauty parlours cut and slice and mould,
Anorexic fantasy of never growing old.
We eat and drink, are merry, rejoicing in our sins,
Overweight and happy; three cheers for double chins!

Cathy Pemberton

A HELPING HAND

The poet toiled throughout the night,
he ignored his waiting bed;
his ideas put all sleep to flight
but the words stayed in his head.

He disdained sleep, like the night birds,
in a way, masochistic;
he wished he had a way with words,
or even was linguistic.

The pen began to take on life,
sped across the empty page;
phrases with sharpness of a knife,
and a bubbling, restless rage.

It was as if another hand
was guiding his cold fingers;
he couldn't start to understand,
but wonderment still lingers.

Imagination runs amok
when one's only half awake;
but words were written on the block,
as the dawn began to break.

Critics called it inspiration,
his star had not been brighter;
but he knew the acclamation
should be for his ghost-writer.

James Kimber

FOREVER IN YOUR HEART

How will you know me as the years go by
No one stays the same, no matter how they try
My youth will long have slipped away
Left there in the shadows from another day

You won't forget me, you tell me so
Those things of me you say you will know
You say you will know my touch
Know the smile you love so much
Know my gentle loving way
Forever in your heart, they'll stay

If I don't make it, don't know what I'll do
Would you ask the Lord, please, just to let me through
I'm sure he knows my love was good and true
And that there was never anyone but you

It won't be long until you say your last goodbye
It's then, the tears will fall like rain, from you and I
To be left with just a memory, of what used to be
How two hearts beat as one, in perfect harmony.

Karl Jakobsen

YIPPEE . . . I SEE

The music blares out loud and free
I stretch up straight but I'm too small to see
My hero on stage? 'It just can't be'
I catch a glimpse and burst with glee
I dreamed for this day to happen to me
I'll keep it locked away in memory
For Ozzy Osbourne I would swim the coldest sea
Or climb to the top of the highest tree
Now Black Sabbath I never miss on TV
He's the king of rock and I've seen him - *whoopee* . . .

Stacey Tully

COUNTRY SOUNDS KNOW NO BOUNDS

Listen to the screeching of the owls around the chimney cowls
The noise of the slugs and the bugs against which
No vegetable patch is a match.
Whilst the crow caws in the straw
Listen to the racket of the rooks in the stooks.
Like the clatter of chattering kids cascading down staircases.

See the scowl of the owl on his perch in the church,
As he looks for his dinner amongst sinners.
Although some mice would be nice
No doubt he will have to make do
With a leetle beetle or two, tu-whit tu-whoo!
To leave the last words to the birds
Would be absurd and frankly, faintly, quaintly.

In the stream, the dace takes its place
In the heart of the race
On the silent approach, of
The silvery roach whilst the curmugenous gudgeon
Leave in a dudgeon to the grumbling rumble
Of the ill-mannered thunder as
Lightning cuts asunder the still of the night.
It is in the still of the night
When the day's cacophony is done
And the light of the harvest moon
Is flooding into your room.
That you can reach up and touch
The silver tenor of the sky and
Listen to its tune, maybe accompanied by the breeze in the trees
And the screeches of the owls in the chimney cowls.

Jack Major

IF ONLY

If only life was simple, no knots to ravel or unfold
If only hair stayed the colour of blonde or simply gold
If only our looks never changed, no creases, spots or wrinkles
If only the stars at night permanently twinkled
If only we could eat a meal just once a day
If only I could wash up once and put the pots away
If only married couples could share the family chores
If only they could give and take and not to become bores
If only they tried to live a better life
If only they could stay the course and last as man and wife
If only we knew when we were born what life we had in store
If only when we die we could come back and visit our loved ones,
                                          just once more.

Pamela Wild

HAUNTED SHORE

In melancholy mist of morning, on the sea,
Grey silhouettes of phantom ships, adrift;
The remnants of their tattered sails float free
As, with the changing breeze, their courses shift:
The lingering shades of those who passed this way
Treading a broken path, through splintered stones
Time has hollowed out their memory
And bleached the scattered fragments of their bones:
Brief hour of glory, bright the flame
That burns away, so soon, to cold, grey ash:
A lonely, rough-hewn tomb that bears no name
Still bears a silent witness to the past:
Yet, in the darkest, bleakest hour of night
The soul may find a secret, hallowed way
To steer a course towards a beacon bright -
And, gently drifting, reach a tranquil bay

Leyna Brinkmeyer

RULERS AND SUFFERERS: THE CHALLENGE

In Sri Lanka, people of two popular cultures, both somewhat similar
As seen by the west, slay one another with guns, bombs and arson.
In Ireland, folks of two strands of the very same faith and culture
As seems to eastern eyes, keep fighting for some sombrous reason.
In both cases who must bear the blame? Their 'democratic' rulers!

In Ethiopia, precious lives from a glorious ancient civilisation
Are lost, not through laziness or war, but through nature's droughts.
In the Middle East, their oil-rich cousins indulge in wars of attrition
In the names of their sects and clans for selfish power-linked 'rights'.
Who should be accused? Indeed again their governments and rulers!

The east produces much less food than enough for its masses to feed,
Due to floods, or lack of water, finance, peace, and organised work.
Westerners mass-produce food through science, more than they need,
And bury or burn their surpluses, lest their balance of economies jerk.
Who should have mended this gaffe? Surely, our UN rule-makers!

To feed their families, millions seek some form of work somewhere,
But millions of others shun work, living on doles, booze and drugs.
Some shed tons of tears for ailing animals and trees, in seeming care;
Some have no more tears left for kids and kin killed by warring thugs.
Whose burden is it to bolster peace and justice in any land? Its rulers'.

In some countries, Taj Mahals are built by their billionaire families
While their fellow citizens can find little to eat or to hide their nudity.
Some men who change women, like clothes, fill columns in dailies
But women living alone are made victims of 'macho' masculinity.
Who must care for and protect all people alike? Indeed their rulers!

I conclude: Our world is in turmoil because many of our era's rulers,
Except, yes, in a few fair countries, are poorly pathetic as leaders!

Kopan Mahadeva

STILL LEARNING

Knowledge is godly, it helps us be free,
It helps understand the things that we see.
It helps understand the troubles of mind,
It helps us break down the monotonous grind.
But knowledge has pitfalls, I'll tell you this,
For knowledge is hurtful, ignorance is bliss.
For knowing betrayal by that of a friend,
Or knowing someone is not on the mend.
By knowing your family will one day be gone,
And you're not immortal, you won't carry on.
So some days the knowing is not as you wish,
But life is not served on a gold plated dish.

Geoffrey Woodhead

FEELINGS

I love to tell you how I feel
Deep down inside my heart
The only bit I don't like
Is when we are apart

I love to lie upon the bed
And feel your naked skin
So soft and gentle next to mine
What ecstasy I'm in

You say I'm always in your heart
And you too are in mine
It's like a perfect fairy tale
We'll share for all of time

I love for us to be alone
In the early hours
When I am overcome with all
My strong and loving powers

We work through any problems
Together hand in hand
For we are both united
Each other we understand

I'm always looking forward
To the future for we two
Because for me there is no doubt
There's no one else but you.

Sue Dalby

What's News

Each day in the papers
We look to read the news,
But now the adverts own more space,
Than the crosswords have got clues.

And puzzled by it all,
The newspapers have become
Large and 'thick',
But there's little now,
Between the pages,
Which really tells us all
What makes the world 'tick'.

Bakewell Burt

CONTEMPLATION

The children have gone back to school today.
The house seems empty, without them at play.
No more toys littering the floor,
Silent the garden, except for the crow's caw.

Sat with my breakfast, toast and tea.
Contemplating my day till three.
When once more they will pour through the door,
Shouting and dropping their bags on the floor.

So what shall I do for the next six hours?
Just sit here and look at the flowers,
Or go down to the shops, and money spend,
Perhaps have coffee and cakes with a friend.

Suppose that I had better housework do,
Or hubby will come home and take a dim view.
If breakfast pots are still in the sink,
He will throw a paddy and kick up a stink.

So now I've got to roll up my sleeves
Haven't time to spend as I please.

G W Bailey

A STORMY SEA

Bashing and crashing the waves go,
and long ago the cargoes came,
all the same.

Lashing waves, and the seaman
braves stormy weather instead of
heather moors, the seaman gets his stores.

Lonely the night in the pale moonlight,
the ships go to and fro, to and fro
- how they go.

Jane Byers

A Memorable Visit

On Saturday, September first, a party visited Rose.
A maiden aunt, an old school friend? Whom do you suppose?
Not a person, but Rose Castle, a most imposing pile
Which is the very beautiful home of the Bishop of Carlisle.

There we were met by the gardener who showed us all around
The gardens, the orchard, and surrounding parkland ground,
Finishing at the tower, which some climbed to the top to stare
At the scenery, while the rest took the evening air.

We were then invited indoors for a welcome cup of tea,
Then upstairs to the Chinese Room and a potted history.
Three very large bay windows give light to this hall of fame,
Showing the unique wall covering which gives the room its name.

Next we went to the Chapel for a service of evening prayer;
Just a simple spoken service, but it seemed so special there.
The Chapel, newly-painted, was looking its very best;
In that little house of God I felt a most privileged guest.

We trooped downstairs to the kitchen to a buffet selection;
We took our plates to the dining room. The meal was just perfection.
After good conversation round the table we then made our way
To buy a souvenir to remind us of this lovely day.

We spent the last hour in the Chapel in discussion and prayer,
Lighting loved ones candles, writing prayers of things for
which we care.
Never has an hour been more enjoyable and gone by so fast,
And I came away from 'Rose' with thoughts that will forever last.

Marlene Allen

YOUNG HEADS

Clear horizons, points of view,
And no confusion of the tongue,
A readiness for something new,
Inspire the wisdom of the young.

Where older heads will stall and freeze,
And let the moment pass,
The opportunities are seized
By younger hands and fast.

All contradictions must be solved,
Not shelved and under-rated.
Observers must become involved,
Opinions out and stated.

For stirring songs are seldom sung
Without the wisdom of the young.

Paul Heinowski

THE VALUE OF LOVE

If love could be bought,
Would you buy some for me?
Would you value it more,
If love wasn't free?
    Would you buy some for birthdays,
    And Christmas time too?
    And hope someone else
    Will buy some for you?
When you open the box,
You will know love is there,
By the way that your partner
Has wrapped it with care.
    For love is a treasure,
    A wonderful gift,
    It makes you feel happy,
    And gives you a lift.
And if you should get some,
Just spread it around,
For it can not be bought,
And it can not be found.
    Love has to be given,
    By someone who cares,
    They don't have to tell you,
    You'll know when it's there.
By the way they treat you,
And the things that they do,
They don't want to hurt you,
Or make you feel blue.
    When you know that you're loved,
    It just sets you free,
    If you have some to spare,
    Would you save it for me?

James Stanley

MASTER KEY

Who holds the master key
to all the many doors
in life's chaotic house
of class-dividing floors,
or is there no such key
with which to liberate
those locked in poverty?

Will any mortal clutch
the master key of peace
and use it to unlock
the doors to man's release,
or will nobody find
the key to harmony
and justice for mankind?

Can any soul on earth
devise a master key
to free imprisoned minds
from constant agony,
or must their spirits wait
for death to proffer them
the key to heaven's gate?

Iaian W Wade

SAME OLD, SAME MOULD

Everybody on the treadmill, wishing they were back in bed still,
Instead of plodding on with workaday routine;
Suffering the morning blues while trapped in traffic queues,
Mile after mile, sat inside a tin machine.
Shiny shoes and High Street suits, make-up applied, dyed roots -
Jobbing faces worn in the early morning gloom,
As yawning heads go bobbing by, a shadow under every eye
That's weary and bleary with rheum.
Downing endless plastic coffees round the clock in every office,
Faxing endless sheets of paper nobody will read;
Answering other people's calls (an occupation that soon palls)
When all you truly want is to be freed.
Ties and collars choking necks as we earn our monthly cheques,
Strips of gaudy cloth with no real use;
Just another way of keeping office workers' hearts from leaping
In case one of them should break loose.
Like mice upon a spinning wheel (minus the rodents' zeal)
Round the calendar we blindly toil;
Performing seals in a circus for the executives that work us -
A mystery worthy of Conan Doyle.
This we do to earn a wage until we reach retirement age,
When at last to pasture we are led;
Once there we go from being drones to wizened OAPs and crones
Dribbling dears mostly daft in the head.
Then we'll wonder what a pity, back when we were young and pretty,
Why we didn't take a pause for thought,
And realise there are better ways of spending all our salad days
Than being underpaid and overwrought.

Jonathan Goodwin

A PRAYER

Dear Lord, if only I could join the throng -
And walk the roads *you* walked upon.
Would I stand in wonder and gaze,
Then listen to your tales - that still amaze?
Watch your tender healing of the sick -
Performed by you, a no mean trick
Would I be speechless in silent awe
See the thousands on the shore -
Who were fed by you, from fish and bread.
You who could simply raise the dead.
Your hands perform miracles - heal the blind
If only I could see your eyes so kind
I would be blinded and turn away,
For I need so much to learn and pray.
Your words repair my wounded soul,
I need your love, to make my spirit whole.
I know you are my friend in need,
You suffered for us, that all may be freed.
We thank you Lord, for your love for us,
Be with us now, in life's headlong rush.

Amen

Dorothy Parish

WHERE HAVE THEY BEEN

These hands, where have they been?
Holding a hospital jug ready to go,
Tanned callused split, not clean.

Aged skin, smoothed prints, what have they seen?
Giving life taking life I just don't know,
These hands, where have they been?

Not a surgeon's dentist's or chef's, not clean
Enough to mend a molar, stitch a toe,
Tanned callused split, not clean.

Create a soufflé, fill a tureen,
More manual drive a tractor push a hoe,
These hands, where have they been?

Father's hands, memories seen
Memories gone, he was an artist long ago,
Tanned callused split, not clean.

Skull pain returns too keen
To think and philosophise, that I know.
These hands, where have they been?
Tanned callused split, not clean.

Roger W Chamberlain

LIVE PEACE!

O where on earth can peace be found,
With wars and fighting all around?
It seems that peace from life has fled,
And peace is only for the dead!

'Lord, may he rest in peace,' we say
When someone dear has passed away;
But that is not the peace we seek,
And sigh and work for, week by week.

Peace is not something we can make,
Peace-keepers' missions undertake
To keep warring factions apart,
But cannot give them peace of heart.

Peace may by won, but at the price
Of pain, tears, and self-sacrifice.
Only when pride and hatred cease
Can we enjoy true, lasting peace.

Peace is more than an end to strife,
Peace is God's harmony in life,
Which comes from loving and forgiving,
And seeking good for all the living!

Nancy Solly

FLIGHTS TO HEAVEN

I like to ride on a steam train
But wonder what it's like in a plane
Flying the sky and back again
Little birds in sun and rain.

A bird flaps its wings again and again
Flies from city lands in country lane.
His journey never in vain
He goes far on a beak of grain.

I'm riding my bike to ease the strain
Going to the station to meet the train
Sit on the platform, watch a flying plane
Feed the birds then back again.

I'll have my wings when I've no pain
You know what I mean - why explain
No need to fly in a plane
When with my wings I'll fly home again.

Ann Weavers

FUNNY THING, THE WIND!

The wind is like glass, transparent and clear.
No time and no season, it's there all the year.
As a breeze in the summer, gently swaying the trees.
As a gale, playing havoc with ships on the seas.
As whirling tornadoes, as violent typhoons,
Rearranging vast deserts into lofty sand dunes.
As a deafening hurricane, as a mighty monsoon,
It whoops and it whooshes while singing its tune.

Yet the wind can be helpful - mischievous as well,
Just what its mood will be no one can tell.
It sends children's kites hurling high in the sky,
With ladies' loose bonnets flying nearly as high!
Across wide open spaces, through crevices small,
The wind knows no bounds - it will explore them all.
Into houses, through cracks, it will whistle and waft.
'Pull the door to,' says Mother. 'There's a terrible draught.'
Funny thing, the wind!

Jade & Alf Nicholles

IN RETROSPECT

If I have wooed
With scant success,
I've overplayed my hand,
I guess.

Suppose I'd played
The waiting game.
Would life have
Turned out just the same?

Or if fate's wheel
Had clicked around
To - *wedded bliss* -
Might I be found,
An ageing prey
To constant care,
With youngsters getting
In my hair?

So if I've wooed
With scant success,
Perhaps it's just as well!
I guess . . .

Donald Harris

COMPASSION'S ROBES

O, man, when will you wear compassion's robes,
Not just self-interest but the globe's,
A suffering world awaits your hand,
Please try to feel, to understand.

You've learned to build and to destroy,
Self-seeking sought to gain, enjoy,
At the expense of souls and lands,
As empires fell like shifting sands.

The time has come to grow, mature,
To your soul-illness find a cure,
The time has come to love and share,
With other beings, everywhere.

That all together we may build,
Conflict's passions calmed and stilled,
A world of joy for each to thrive,
For this grand goal we all must strive.

Emmanuel Petrakis

AN ILLUSION

Magnificent avenue of tall stately trees
Bending, stretching gently in light breeze
Winds strengthening, tall trees now behave
Like tall sail ships battling against mighty wave

In far distant horizon beyond the avenue
Dark, silent, menacing mountains come into view
Silhouetted against blazing colours of setting sun
Daylight fast retreating, another day is done

Shadowing images projected on misty peaks
Black predatory creature his last meal seeks
Mirrors of light creating illusion of immense space
Moonbeams distorting mountain's face

Rushing mountain waters tumbling over stone
Waterfall silvered by pale magical moonlight
Water sprites hoping they are alone
Dancing sprightly through the beams of light

Fallacy of vision, optical illusion
False images, unreal conclusion
What joy the gift of imagination
Appreciating mysteries of such creation

K G Johnson

RHYME

When my thoughts conjure up poetry they turn straight to rhyme.
The only reason I can give is that it was rampant in my time.
I've tried many another form,
But to me rhyming verse is the norm.
It is not easy to find the right word,
But you sit thinking and it flutters to mind suddenly - like any bird.
Make a note of it - for you see,
If you don't it might just flee.

Betty Green

TIME

Time comes with passing -
Of minutes, hours and days,
So coming through different centuries -
Which all have their different ways.

Time is about birthdays -
Which transpires every year,
A time to get together -
With those we hold most dear.

Time never rushes -
But goes on at its own pace,
Teaching us to be orderly -
And keeping things in place.

Our lives evolve through time,
Where so much we can learn,
So aim to keep in step with time,
So success we can earn.

Rachael Marshall (10)

THE MUSIC MAKERS

We are the music makers
We wander by the sea
We sit on south coast beaches
We sing our songs with glee.

Composing endless ditties
Combining endless screams
Countless rhyming lyrics
Canned psychedelic dreams.

We get our inspiration
We listen to the tide
Wet rollers bash the shingle
While we stare goggle-eyed.

Sometimes we write a hit tune
Some people think we're grand
So platinum can't last that long
Sad loss in life's quicksand.

So even if we write a flop
Surely what we have do
Sit down on the beach and play
Until our dream comes true.

We are the music makers
We play by night and day
We know you must have heard our songs . . .
You have? Well, that's okay.

Frank Ede

A CURLY TALE

In January 'Ninety-Eight
Two ginger piggies cheated fate.
To be pork chops they weren't too keen;
A rasher pair you've never seen.
They looked around the abattoir
And soon decided they were far
From happy with the schemes of man
And so devised a cunning plan:

Butch Cassidy and Sundance Pig
Broke out into the world so big
And when they'd swum the river wide
Stood dripping on the other side.
They crossed the field and soon they both
Were crackling through the undergrowth.
Life on the run was tough, of course,
But better this than apple sauce!

The papers followed for a week
The saga of their hide and seek
And television showed their plight;
Beamed round the earth by satellite.
Such a lot of risks they'd taken;
Lying low to save their bacon.
But hunger served to show them how
It wasn't worth a sausage now.

Worn out with being on the run
The pigs surrendered one by one.
But plans to kill them came to nought;
Their owner said, 'Now they've been caught
They'll have a check-up at the vets
And live their lives as pampered pets.'
Fair reward for causing laughter
They'll be happy ever after.

Dennis W Turner

FLOWER POWER

Oh dear a me,
What a flower I be,
Two young men came a courting me.
One was blind, the other couldn't see,
Oh dear a me what a flower I be.

Bernard Booth

BODY AND SOUL

She liked to write a bit
But now she's had enough of it.
Now she can rest all the day
Until the winds do blow away
Do blow away the winds of time
And no more thinks of words to rhyme
But helps to push the daisies up
The bluebells too, and buttercup
And dwells among ethereal bowers
And is now, the fragrance of the flowers.

Constance I Roper

THE BRAIN OPERATOR

He sits alone
In a pure white coat
Surrounded by monitors
Keeping things afloat
Camera nine isn't working
Something must be wrong
He phones the man in charge
To ask what's going on
'Just a technical fault'
Comes back the man's reply
'Then sort it out,' shouts the operator
He shakes his head and sighs
Everything is functioning
Up, down, round and around
Clicking, tapping as it moves
All a familiar sound
Signals being sent
For you to move your head
Next you have a yawn
Something tells you it's time for bed
The operator can close down now
Puts the monitor on automatic
He chooses a dream for you
Tonight - nothing too dramatic
He leans back in his chair
Checking things are okay
He's now retiring for the night
It's been such a busy day

Joanne H Hale

MY ADVENTURE BOOK

Life is an adventure book. It starts at chapter one.
When I receive forgiveness and trust in God's dear son.

Chapter two is wonderful. I've been granted a new start,
And people see the change in me, now Christ reigns in my heart.

I'm spending many hours in prayer, now this is chapter three,
And learning from God's precious word, how Christians ought to be.

Chapter four goes quickly - I am busy, but content,
Serving in my local church with gifts from Heaven sent.

Chapter five sees illness - dark clouds hang overhead
It's now I know His presence whatever lies ahead.

'I will never leave you, or forsake you,' Jesus says
And now that I'm at chapter six, I'm back to brighter days.

The middle chapters of my book are like a travel guide.
I've been to many countries, yet still He's by my side.

There is a special section, which I devote to prayer,
For those outside the kingdom, who never seem to care.

Some are in my family - how I long to see the day,
When they come to faith in Jesus, who has washed their sin away.

The Christian life is thrilling, when the master's in control.
That's why I think it's like a book and I can play my role.

There may be many chapters left, or maybe just a few.
So I put my trust in Jesus - it's the best thing I can do.

And when this book is finished, I'll start another one.
Recording my adventures in the presence of God's son.

J Smyth

JUMBLE SALE

I'm a jumble sale addict
They are really good fun
Lots of bargains for everyone
Outside the doors the crowds are gathered
Then the sale begins and they all surge in
Rushing to find bargains galore
Then looking again and buying some more
Everyone has a good rummage through
To see what there is that will surely do
There's always a very good bookstall indeed
So you're sure to find something you would like to read
There are always some toys and puzzles too
So you might find a jigsaw you'd like to do
Then take a look at the bric-a-brac stall
With all sorts of things to appeal to all
You might find a lovely picture or a very pretty vase
Handbags and kitchen things and a selection of jars
Something you are wanting may just be there
So look through all the bargains with plenty of care
Then there is the linen stall, more bargains to be had
Bedspreads and tablecloths and cushion covers too
Or you might find some curtains just to suit you
Once I got a lovely dress for only thirty pence
I snapped it up quickly before it went
So if you want a bargain that's going cheap
Go to a jumble sale and you may find
The very thing you had in mind.

S C Talmadge

THE LORD IS KING

When shadows fall on another day
fading the light, when bright stars appear,
to dance upon the velvet way,
that tells me God is near.

When the sun is risen, in the eastern sky
with warm rays, gay to see.
When dewdrops kiss the early rose
then I feel that God is here.

When birdsong echoes through forests green
and is heard far overland
I feel God's grace can there be seen
with a touch of a father's hand.

When rivers flow, and oceans sing
when we glimpse the wonders each season brings
they all tell me
that my Lord is king.

Jean Parry

STARLING JOY

You are my life, my breath, my starling joy,
  My pleasures, and my cares,
When watching you my spirits buoy,
  Released of cruel despairs.

Oh! I could stay here and sit,
  Sojourning lonesome for a while,
Listening to your banterous wit,
  And smirk a broadening smile.

When the clean air is dry and hot
  You gather round a pool and prattle,
Self-consciousness is soon forgot,
  When wading, you splash and paddle.

Mighty Aphrodite's feathered flowers
  You provide a chirping distraction,
Diverting our gaze in sun and showers
  With the sheer gaiety of your action.

Skipping about I've seen you running,
  Revelling in your pranks and play,
Living as though the end were coming
  And this was to be your last day.

Clustered in groups, patrolling in pairs,
  Lively, exuberant, or shrinkingly coy -
Realised are all my hopes and prayers,
  Buoyed by a tide of starling joy.

Heys Stuart Wolfenden

CASKET OF JEWELS

Lift the lid of the casket
I am blinded with light
Like the stars that shine
On a dark, frosty night

Shafts of light dancing
From one to another
On a beautiful bracelet
Which belonged to my mother

Diamonds so precious
None can compare
Why here is a slide
I once wore in my hair

Beautiful cameo crafted so fine
Is a special favourite of mine
Pearls like teardrops on a silver thread
Came from the deepness of the seabed

Sapphires as blue as the deepest lagoon
Must have them valued again very soon
Rubies that burn with the hottest of fires
Are always the joy of man's desire

Crystals reflecting colours anew
Red and purple, green and blue
A gold wedding ring from me to you

Not just a casket of material things
But a host of memories which a happy life brings

Vicki Harrold

WORDS

It brings a certain pleasure to my mind
That written words defy the law of time
To leave a little part of me behind.

To waxing lyrical I am inclined
For poetry, to me, must be in rhyme.
It brings a certain pleasure to my mind.

If in the future somebody should find
Some words composed by me when in my prime
To leave a little part of me behind

Then I've achieved the goal for which I signed,
For words can last longer than clocks will chime,
It brings a certain pleasure to my mind.

To take my final bow I am resigned
For I've known some successes in my climb.
It brings a certain pleasure to my mind
To leave a little part of me behind.

Joy Saunders

LITTLE HANDS

In life, let the little children be a blessing of one's love,
hold them in your heart, share their tears and sorrow.
Wipe away the pain and see the peace of a dove
descend on the face of a child, a smile replacing furrow.
Then walk in the meadow where grass and wildflower stand,
feel the glow of a child's love as you feel your finger held
with a little hand.
You look down and a smile comes that says I love you,
no words can describe a tug of the heart, a feeling so new.
A parent will tell you there is nothing so grand,
in life, than to feel the touch of a little child's hand.

John Clarke

BUTTERFLIES

Butterflies are flitting by,
The sun is shining in the sky.
They fly and land on every flower,
Make the most of every hour.
Such a pretty sight to see,
As it flutters past the tree.
Spreads its wings to catch the sun,
Before the fading day is done.

Betty Mason

NATURE'S LANDSCAPE

Eagles plummeting down from their lofty nest.
A half-hidden rabbit stops to rest.
Widespread pinions produce a whining sound,
Seizing its victim from the ground!

The mother shoves her offspring into the air!
Struggling, plunging, anxious care!
The parent's rescue has always begun,
Until the two will fly as one!

Wispy clouds draped around mountainous heights,
Softly caressing heavenly sights.
Rocky majesties, forgotten by time.
Gnarled statues tempt bravehearts to climb!

Cascading waterfalls leaping down.
Glistening in their pure white gown.
Rushing drops descend to coolest places.
Spraying mist onto watchers' faces!

Cool caverns conceal their fairy story.
Stony icicles wrapped in glory!
Underground palaces made without tools.
Glistening princess, flaunting her jewels!

Stately pines stand guard by the silent lake.
Green-clad sentries must stay awake!
Outstretched arms want to ward off invasion,
Cherishing this peaceful occasion!

All of life bound together by nature's rope.
Leaves exhaling their future hope.
A magnificent landscape, painted pure.
May humans help it to endure!

Val Spall

MY IDEA OF HEAVEN

Magic perfume fills the air,
Scent of roses everywhere,
Summer sunshine, skies of blue,
A bonus is the lovely view.

Little children, cute and sweet,
Fractious in the summer heat,
Old folks sit and take a rest,
The girls show off their summer best.

Everyone is feeling good,
Summer sunshine sets the mood,
Enjoy your life, admire the flowers,
Enjoy the minutes and the hours.

Sweet music drifting on the air,
Relax, enjoy it free from care,
Life is good you must agree,
Appreciate it all, it's free.

Margaret Lynch

THE HAUNTING

Wandering down a street with no name
The battered scenery still looks the same
To a bruised and painful eye
That has made me stop and question why
An individual has to always fight
For that rare glimpse of holy light

Bloodied hand resting upon my shoulder
Its grip gets stronger as I grow older
Leaving a stain that never washes away
A permanent reminder of a darker day
Nearing the avenue, my eyes reluctantly roam
Towards the ghost that was last year's home

Exasperated by feelings of what could've been
I'm trapped inside a bittersweet dream
Where once happiness and the sound of laughter
Filled the air with happy ever after
But it's a broken dream to which I now cling
Those once joyous voices now refuse to sing

P D Wade

THE MAGIC OF RHYMING

Whoever said rhyming was out of fashion
And definitely old hat
Has never been seized by a rhyming passion
Could it be his soul is flat?
To amble along in a non-rhyming way
Is an easier thing by far,
But oh the thrill of the rhyming one
On his quest for a rhyming star.
The joy he feels when *that word* appears
He has searched for hard and long,
How he writes it down with exultant tears
Interspersed with jubilant song.
Let verse-makers today go plodding along
With their flat pedantic prose,
But oh I can say with all my heart
I could never be one of those.
For me the lilt of the dancing rhyme
Is a thing to forever cherish
And should it ever be thoughtlessly banned
Then the life of the poem would perish.

Margaret Rose Harris

MY WORLD

When it's night-time and I go to bed
There's a place I go to in my head
In an instant all my dreams come true
I can be who I want to and do what I choose

I can be a princess wearing a long, flowing gown
Upon my head sits a sparkling crown
Or ride through the lands, a gallant knight
Upon my trusty steed of snowy white

Lands filled with dragons, giants and dwarves
Goblins and witches and wizards galore
Lands filled with magic, of mysteries untold,
Lands of adventure, of treasure and gold

I can be a pirate sailing a lemonade sea
Eating ice cream for breakfast, dinner and tea
In a world with marshmallow mountains and lollipop trees
Only in my world this place do I see

In summer I can have Christmas day
And ride with Santa on his sleigh
Past the moon and twinkling stars
Better than any motor car

I can make it day or I can make it night
I can make it whatever time of year I like
I can make the snow fall or make the sun shine
But, whatever I choose, the choice is mine

So, at night, when you're a sleepyhead
And you lie all snug and warm in bed
Let your imagination fly, set it free
And you will visit this place, like me

Vanessa Bell

THE SALES PROMOTER

You walk the alien streets until their greyness taints your soul,
As end to end and endlessly they lead to some blind goal
That you may not even recognise, may never be aware
You can reach a destination, to find there's nothing there.
The high streets of the provinces seem all to look the same,
And you lose all identity, no face, no voice, no name.

The dust lies in the gutters in the summer's sultry heat,
Or winter rains make pavements darkly shine beneath your feet.
But this you scarcely notice, and the crowds that hurry by,
Are not of people, but consumers, each with ratings, low or high,
And the cities are statistics to be plotted on a chart,
With every fluctuation, like the beatings of a heart.
The red lines are the losses and the blue lines are the gains,
They are woven deep within you, like arteries and veins.

As you walk the city streets upon your solitary crusade,
Your mind revolves round innovative ways for boosting trade.
In the past you've increased profits by spectacular amounts,
But in sales, today's performance is the only one that counts.
When blue lines soar up skywards, with the brightest stars you shine,
But when they start to falter, your job is on the line.

At times you feel a strange malaise, not easily defined,
And make a resolute attempt to drive it from your mind.
The one who claims to love you is a long way from this place,
Sometimes you close your eyes and you cannot visualise his face,
And you feel that you must see him, but it's just an idle dream,
With the end of season's sales ahead, and the new commission scheme.
Incentives and percentages and classified dissections,
Target figures, display themes, and surplus stock inspections.

The red lines are the losses, the blue lines are the gains,
In the midst of life's complexities, this simple fact remains.
So let the blue lines curve up strongly while the red lines dip down low,
Here's the best life has to offer. Here is all you need to know.

M Mettam

POEMS ON THE TRAIN

Writing poems on the train,
What a way to tax the brain.
Does it scan and does it rhyme?
No it doesn't, all the time!
Write of rhyme - rumpty tum
Writer of boredom - numb the bum
Write of twittering - please be dumb
Write of dreaming - kingdom come.

When I write with hand a-shake,
Smell of diesel, smell of brake,
Words staccato form in line,
Tense of shoulder, curved of spine.
All ideas round trains assemble
Pen and paper both a-tremble,
Ideas short as track is long
Station comes to end my song.

Laptops hum and mobiles ring,
Why ever do they bring the thing?
Louts a-shouting, workers snore,
Who could ever beg for more?
Journey's ending, almost here,
Had enough to last a year,
But tomorrow, ten to eight,
I'll be back, unless it's late.

David W Lankshear

SUBURBAN ELEGY

And when it closes on its noiseless springs
As soft as felt and just as easily
I'll look back awhile and hope to see
What door it was led me from the life of things

And see not one but many doors the same
All black or brown with darkened windowpane
And through each glass I know I'll look in vain
For some loved or hated or familiar name

And I'll look back awhile and wonder why
Of all the ways it had to be that way
Though which it was I'll fail to say
Being just a wraith without a human eye

And in despair I'll curse my lack of sense
'Wasn't it in life the same' I'll cry
'Never knowing which path I took or why
For the fog about my feet so dark and dense?'

And when it opens on eternity
Leaving me I know not what to face
A hand of retribution or of grace
A Hadean mist descending over me

Then will I clamour like a desperate thing
Lobbying each likely life to let me through
Of beggar, leper, even thief will do
Rather than face that fearful lingering

Then I'll remember each field, each stream
Each long low wall on which pale lilacs hung
Even the paths to which the goose grass clung
So sweet will this dull world seem
A dear disparaged dream
When life puts out her beam.

Sarah Knox

D-I-V-O-R-C-E

My son, he found himself a girl.
She soon had him in a whirl.
Pretty quick, they got engaged and war on their new house, they waged.

House now like an 'Ideal Home',
they sent out invites - for to come
and see their marriage, duly done. Then - off he went! My only son!

Four years later, August time,
a grandchild promised. The first of mine.
Christmas passed . . . then March '88, Sarah arrived. 7.2 in weight.

Christmas came with games and toys.
I wondered, 'What'd suit little boys?'
In August came a sad, sad day, as plans they made, to move away!

January, the deeds they sign -
and went to live in number nine.
July - the atmosphere was bad and both of them seemed very sad.

September, in the park, she said,
'It's really coming to a head.'
October then. My son moved out, lives and loves in so much doubt.

November, to the law they went -
discussed divorce! An ugly event!
What happened to our special couple? Why did their cherished
dreams all topple

in this cruel and wicked way?
I - for one - just cannot say.
Their parting seems in undue haste and leaves behind it -
so much waste!

D-i-v-o-r-c-e is just another word
often spoken, often heard.
Oh! Why does it happen? Time after time? Why! Oh! Why!
Did it happen to mine?

Joyce Dobson

A VISIT TO THE DOCTOR'S

As we sit in the Doctor's waiting room
Everyone's face is full of gloom
It will be a long wait, by the look
Of the man over there reading his book.

Then a voice crackles loudly out of the speaker
Has the thing gone wrong, or my hearing getting weaker.
I couldn't hear whether he said Jane or James
When trying to read out the patient's names.

Through the door another patient would walk
An acquaintance, who would want to talk.
So keep on chatting, I'll give her a smile
If she sees we're together it will cramp her style.

Children get fidgety and start playing about
Their mother is cross and wants to shout.
It's your turn next, I hear them call
I'll go outside and wait by the wall.

Lynne Walden

TRIOLET

Where is the scheme,
Those words that fit?
That is my dream.
Where is the scheme?
Past, point your beam,
Help me grasp it.
Where is the scheme?
Those words that fit.

Julie Longman

1999 BC

Sometimes it's difficult to understand
This situation was never planned
Although discord is difficult to mend
I cherish you more than any friend
You can't possibly really know
How much this hurts and pains me so
Now you're gone and I am here
Periodically shedding a lonely tear
For every tear that stains my face
Others fall to take its place
I lie alone at night in bed
Thoughts of you swirling round my head
Often I wish my heart would die
No more I'd need to sit and cry
As I sit here feeling low
There's something I want you to know
My love runs deep and must be told
My feelings are nigh impossible to control
You made me feel a colossal fool
I finally blew it and lost my cool
What event is worth being so silly
To risk what I shared with you Billy
Now I want to scream and shout
Don't let friendship die in the fallout
Although you're with her instead of me
I'll love you through eternity
I'm sorry if this makes you mad
But sometimes I feel so very sad
I wish we could take a few steps back
Before everything went out of whack

Moira H Thorburn

WAS IT SO

Trill, trill ye lark o'er Farham Park, thy floating ardour flow
On mansion wall, and waterfall, where hart, and sweetheart go,
Trill, trill thine airs, thy sylvan wares,
As I in wonder stand and stares -
'Mid apple groves, and plums and pears -
Thine effervescence show.
Whilst chestnuts, stately dancing, flares,
And warming winds do blow.

O rustic rime of morning time, all in thy summ'ry shade,
Wast ever whelmed more beautiful upon this garden glade.
I stay to while the early day,
As rabbits in the paddock play,
And blackbirds probe, and tit and jay -
Their fleeting moments made.
The native earth in richness lay -
In ev'ry vibrant blade.

O solitude, art rough and rude, under the willow tree -
The cataract leaps splendidly, like thunder of the sea.
And playfully she falls and breaks -
On silver boulders, silver lakes,
And sneaks away, ten thousand snakes -
Of rippling unity.
And thither is, the fisher takes
His quarry home for tea.

Ah was it so, so long ago, so haunting as ye seem,
Ye banks that bloom wi' flowering, art throes of ancient's dream.
Ye fruitful valleys, plots and pound,
Pastoral mead, and cottage ground,
Wi' barking dog, wi' cows abound -
Beside the babbling stream.
Hearken, the tabor's glor'ous sound
Athwart my silent dream.

D Haskett-Jones

CHOCOLATE

Taking one square I persuade myself to eat,
I chew it slowly, savouring the chocolately taste.
The flavour remains for a few moments, a treat,
If I don't finish it, it'll go to waste.

The next few squares slip down my throat,
Filling my mouth with delicious chunks.
Eating too quickly for there to be a thick coat,
Not melting, breaking off chunks.

Slowly the weight of the bar is less,
And even less, each bite takes more.
Of course I'm leaving no mess,
I've got to stop, my jaw is becoming sore.

A whole kilogram demolished,
All dieting completely abolished!

Miranda Bentley

LUCKY, LUCKY ME

Thank you God for my eyes
And all that I can see
Thank you God for my sight
Oh lucky, lucky me

Thank you God for every limb
That moves without the need of aid
Treasures that are priceless
Yet I have never paid

Thank you God for my kids
Their lives lived normally
Thank you God for this gift
Oh lucky, lucky me

Thank you God for blood and bone
Not touched with a disease
Thank you God with all my heart
For treasures such as these

Thank you God for I have learned
The best things in life are free
Thank you God for all my world
Oh lucky, lucky me

Deana Freeman

ATOMIC ADAM

'Horror plumed' upon my head:
Bitten apple: world all dead.

At the gate an angel stands:
Phials of fission in his hands.

Nuclear nudes: we all must dress
In paper bags our nakedness,

How original our sin:
Future cancers breed within.

Do you see that spin-stop cloud?
Not a pillar, but a shroud.

Insane all the seasons go:
Summer withers into snow!

Satan's fools we all have been!
Purge our sins with iodine.

Smooth milk, once immaculate,
Sin will soon contaminate.

Womb time weeps for genes beguiled
Turn to monster unborn child.

Eve and I take hands again;
Abel's dead; but where is Cain?

E J Williams

EVERYONE'S A POET

'I don't think writing poems is fun!'
'Well, let's see how it could be done.
What rhymes with cat? Sat, fat and mat
And lots of words that rhyme with at'
'Once I knew a cricketing cat
Who hit mid stump and cried, 'How's that?''
'Let's try again, what about dog?
Hog, log and fog, bog, cog and jog.
Or cow that sat upon a bough
And sang a song, a dreadful row.
Or bluebell blooming in a dell
Lying close to a wishing well.
A great many words rhyme with air,
Some spelt the same and some like care.
And anyway not all must rhyme,
Alternate lines will do just fine.
So you see, it's not very hard,
If you tried, you could be a bard.'

Marjorie Haddon

IF ONLY!

If black was white
And sky was sea
If I were you and you were me
If everything was upside down
If children swam and never drowned
If cars and walls were soft as fluff
If everyone had 'just enough'
If neighbours cared and never strife
If war was peace and death meant life
If guns and knives did not exist
If being killed meant being kissed
If everyone cared for another
If every child had a loving mother
If all the sadness turned to love
If rain fell gently from above
If sun was shared by everyone
If loneliness meant having fun
Then maybe, just maybe
The news would be
That only good things happen, there's no misery!

Lynne Hope

JUPITER, THE BRINGER OF JOLLITY

A giant among giants, weighing 2½ times the other planets together,
the largest of them all in this solar system, no doubt as to whether,
11 times the size of earth, 88,700 miles wide, this is the only one,
a whirling ball of gas, mostly of hydrogen and helium-like the sun,
and 483.6 million miles away from the sun, the 5th planet from it,
Jupiter always takes 11.86 years to make just one solar orbit,
the great swirling red spot is 3 times the size of planet Earth,
and has been spinning and rotating ever since its Jovian birth,
a gaseous globe possibly without a solid surface behind the shade,
the cloud top temperatures of the planet Jupiter are -150°C,
with 13 moons, the two biggest are called Callisto and Ganymede,
both are so huge as to be larger than the planet Mercury indeed,
another moon, Io is the most volcanic in the entire solar system,
revolving between Mars and Saturn, Jupiter, since who knows when.

Christopher Higgins

THE KEY

Walls within walls, dark tunnels of thought,
How many times have escape I sought?
But if I should flee, then where can I go?
Is there freedom above, or freedom below?

Is it days, months or years, how long have I been here,
Living each day, each night with my fear?
Fear of the dark, of the demons within,
The brain's fevered symphony, that cacophonous din.

Locked in this prison, entombed in my own mind,
Is the secret of the freedom I'm attempting to find.
As my demons invade my tortured soul,
So insanity beckons, with a terrible toll.

Who will release me, does anyone care?
Is there hope for one such as me out there?
I know I'll be fine, if they'd just set me free,
But somewhere deep inside, I'm still hiding the key!

Brian L Porter

LOOKING AHEAD

Cross legged I sat upon a cloud
To my dismay I wore a shroud.
A passing angel said to me,
'Perhaps you'd like a cup of tea,
I'm sorry that you have to wait,
Down there has been a massive 'quake'.
So many coming, not yet due
But don't despair, we'll get to you!
What was it brought you here to us,
A car maybe, or country bus?
The reason for your visit's plain
Except of course, there is no pain!
Of course, if 'private' is your style,
You'd jump the queue by many a mile.
It's really not that different here
Unlike on earth, no atmosphere!
Up here of course, your 'really dead'
With time to muse, what lies ahead.
'Rejection', just might be for you
So down to the devil, and friends you knew!'

T G Bloodworth

AUTUMN LIGHT

Now autumn breezes sing of amber light,
    and morning air blows shadows on my face.
Cool crystal stars heed early frosted night,
    the chills of morning push through linen lace.
As barley fields are cropped and set to store,
    the azure skies of evening fade to red.
The liberty of summer locks the door
    and soon to warmer fireside I am led.
Such restless leaves dance lightly on the ground,
    to blow away in final dancing hour.
The treasures of the trees do now abound,
    as fruits and hips and haws replace the flower.
And on the seasons draw through threaded time,
    once more the autumn harvest, so divine.

Hilary Vance

LET BEE

There is an orchid not too proud
to suffer aid (in glades bee-loud)
in pollinating her strange, precious flowers.

And bees debarred wedded bliss
are very fortunate in this -
that they may seek relief from work-long hours

among a mild and generous clan
who do not think that sinful man
(or bee) is *cursed* with sexual relations.

Self-fertile though the orchid is,
she hides her strength and flatters his,
enticing him to break Queen's regulations.

Sometimes on Sabbath Sundays she
both praises God *and* helps the bee . . .

Guy de Chemincreux

FIXING A POEM

To 'fix' a poem, the fixative must be
Of human interest; of love and mystery;
Soft glow of life or darker thoughts on dying -
Melancholy dreams of ageing angels crying;
A plan - a metre; get that foot a-tapping!
Fill the flowing bowl with rough ideas -
Then sift the chaff - discard the wrapping,
Think of lovers' joy, nightmares and fears;
You're half way now to understanding Poesy;
Concentrate on words - call up the muse!
Concentrate your mind; the future's rosy!
Pen to paper - you can do it if you choose;
It's ten to one you'll bore us all to tears,
But thus it's ever been from early years!

Peter Jeevar

MY CAT

First thing in the morning
When I come down the stairs,
I'll get a kiss 'good morning',
Then I'll brush her hair.

Her coat is soft and silky,
A real pleasure to touch,
And when I've done her back and tail,
She wants her tummy brushed.

When she thinks she's had enough
She'll get down off my knee,
And wander into the garden
To get some refreshing breeze.

I don't go out too often,
But my cat seems to know,
She's always waiting at the door
To welcome me back home.

She'll watch as I discard my coat
And then prepare a meal,
Then there will be a quiet miaow
'I'm still here - don't forget me'.

When she thinks she's had enough
She'll settle down to sleep,
Curled up in her basket,
That's when I kiss her good night -
As I take a peep.

Laura D Harris

WHAT I WOULDN'T DO FOR MY MATE BILL

Hold his hand in the playground,
Carry his books to the school gate,
Little Billy Baxter, the boy with one best mate.
One square of chewing gum - split into two,
The bigger bit for me but a piece for Billy too.

I save his place in the dinner line, so Billy pushes in,
It's only a little place coz Billy's only thin,
I got real big muscles and a hair on my chest,
But I still think my mate Bill; well he's the best.
Billy's good at maths, computers and geography too,
I'm only good when Billy's there, he helps me muddle through.

I see what Billy sees and he sees the same as me,
He's good at describing things, it's almost like I can see.
It doesn't really matter to me if I stay the way I am;
As long as Billy doesn't mind being part of my future plan.

I've never seen my mate Bill, I bet he looks real cool:
He's so good at everything especially at school.
He is best at describing things, he brings them to life.
If I were a girl I'd like to become, well . . . Billy's wife!

Janet Millard

FRIENDSHIPS

There are those very good things
That stand out in a life
Places, people, happenings
Children and a wife

There are those you meet in living
Who pass you on the way
A tiny few you treasure
Once met, they always stay

And life is made the richer
For the friendship that you find
The perfect fit of friendships
Are the ying and yang defined

Ray Ryan

THE GENTLE LION

The lion always seems to me
A power-house of energy,
A primitive who looks laid back
Until he's ready to attack.

With regal pride he shakes his mane,
Jealously guarding his domain,
Ever-watchful with feral eye
Lest an usurper should pass by.

But I know one who's not like that -
He's simply not that kind of cat.
He doesn't growl. He doesn't roar.
Such macho noises are a bore!

Unlike his peers who love to fight,
He thinks he has a perfect right
To please himself when stalking prey,
Just looks at it, then walks away.

He doesn't live by jungle law
Which stipulates that tooth and claw
Are necessary to devour
A balanced diet by the hour.

To him all meats taste just the same,
So he declines all bigger game,
And though he favours smaller fare,
He still prefers his viands rare.

When the agile, svelte impala
Leaps across the wide savannah,
He isn't even tempted to
Chase it as other lions do.

Instead you'll often see him lie
With timid fauna nearby,
Resting quietly 'neath the sun,
Feeling at peace with everyone.

Celia G Thomas

BOX IN THE BEDROOM

There's a box in the bedroom full of memories for me
Many years ago I played football you see
The cups that I keep are all that remain
Of the days when I was one of the best in the game.

I take them all out and polish each one
I sit there and think of the day it was won
The days of my youth when I was young and fit
Not like today, I'm too big for my kit.

I still have the memories and the TV of course
I watch all the games and feel a bit of remorse
I never earned the money they get today
But I loved the game and was happy just to play.

Pauline Nind

TOGETHERNESS

I'm sorry you've been away for so long,
Let's get together,
And have a good sing song.

Ann Lacy

IN YOUR SHADOW

I stood in the shadow of you,
But I didn't care.
There was nothing else to do,
But I was happy there.

My role in life was meant to be
A wife, and then a mother,
Our life went on quite happily,
Content with one another.

So, for nearly sixty years,
In good times, or in bad,
We had no time for doubts or fears,
We enjoyed the time we had.

I still say 'ours' and 'us' and 'we',
I've said those words so long,
Can't get used to 'my' and 'mine' and 'me',
Somehow they seem quite wrong.

I do everything in slow motion,
My actions are terribly slow,
Sometimes I haven't a notion
If I should come, or stay, or go.

The people who help me are caring,
They tell me that I'm doing well,
But my 'good days' are getting sparing,
And I'm feeling too tired to tell.

My wish is that I could be there
And free to answer your call,
But I must remain here,
One half of a wonderful whole.

Laura Congreves

TART WITH A HEART

Love them, or hate them, they rule our life,
Give us lots of pleasure but can cause some strife,
The harder they work just makes us smile,
We get bored, so we change them, after a while.

Always someone ready to do a quick swap,
It gets out of hand, when will it stop?
She has a great body, so warm when inside,
Every would-be suitor wants a quick ride.

Some get so jealous when they take her out,
They don't really want her, just show her about,
She is thirsty, but never goes over the top,
Costs me an arm and a leg, she does not stop.

Just like a cat she really does purr,
I would be gutted if I lost her,
She does everything I want her to do,
The moment she does not our romance is through.

You may think I am a chauvinist swine,
But this lady will always be mine,
I use her and abuse her, she does not complain,
She could be lethal if she had a brain.

Ladies, I apologise, please let me explain,
Your sex is safe, so need to complain,
I wash her, pamper her, make her body cleaner,
I am talking about my beautiful Toyota Carina.

Preston M Brooth

As One With You

I want to take you tenderly
enfolded within these protective arms.
As sheltered from the storms of life
while I purge away - all its harms.
Shrouded only in purest honesty
no use for lies or besmudging charms.

To caress your aching limbs
from all their encroaching dread.
While refreshing emotions suppressed
bringing nature's choice to head.
And be as one with you
proving all is true - as said.

A special - enchanted world
created there as just for you.
Where all that's wished becomes reality
and each moment's cherished true.
With sparkling skies of maraudic turquoise
spent always - being as one with you.

Gary J Finlay

PEGGY

Why do men fall at her feet?
I think she's ugly,
And not at all sweet.
Gazes in the mirror like she's a queen,
Her greasy hair she begins to preen.
Plucks out her beard strands one by one,
Rubbing her chin to see if they're all gone.

Looking deep into her crossed eyes,
Yet another suitor on his knees cries.
'Oh Peggy, my Peggy won't you marry me?
I love you my darlin', I'm all lost at sea.'
But she just smiles, revealing two teeth;
Another proposal, it's beyond belief!
Why can't I be lucky like Peg?
I can't get a fella, no matter how much I beg.

Yes, it's true, she's a lottery winner,
But still she could be a little thinner;
Have you seen the size of her hips,
And the way she dribbles and spits?
No, I'm not jealous,
How could I be,
Peggy is my best friend you see!

V Stevens

LOST INNOCENCE

I once knew a child in a seaside town
Whose eyes were blue and hair light brown
Who sang to the sea and danced to the moon
And stirred her tea with a silver spoon.

But this chaste child was taught to choose
Between the fates of win or lose;
Taught to know, despite her song,
The world's made up of right and wrong.

She struggled hard to come to terms
With schools of thought that facts affirm
Found she danced with feet of clay
When time and work denied her play.

She changed her song, she changed her dress
She learnt that life is more or less;
That falls and failures disgrace fools
Who tumble down between two stools.

She turned to the sea and looked at the moon
And lost her childhood all too soon;
But she sang in her sleep and danced in her dreams
Knowing that life was more than it seems.

David Bowes

HOMELAND

As I travel to Ireland across the sea
I dream of days gone by
A peaceful setting awaits me
As I drift under an azure sky

Endless fields of emerald green
Is what I've come here for
Legend abounds in this idyllic place
Passed down from days of yore

The friendly folk who greet me here
Have love in their hearts for me
Away from the bustle of city life
Is the way it ought to be

Philip O'Leary

CHRISTMAS JOY

Come let us all our voices raise
　　And loud the organ play -
With joy we sing, for Christ the king
　　Was born on Christmas day.
Now in a humble manger
　　The Lord of all things lies -
In cattle stall sleeps, weak and small
　　The maker of the skies.

The angels' song that fills the heavens
　　The watching shepherds share,
And hastily they run to see
　　The great good shepherd there.
Then kings come trav'lling from afar
　　To see the child foretold:
Strange gifts they bring this greater king
　　Myrrh, frankincense and gold.

The word now dwells among us
　　The hay His cradle makes;
His home above is left in love -
　　A servant's form He takes.
He comes, a homeless stranger
　　Our pain and grief to share
That we might be from sin set free
　　Safe in His tender care.

Barbara Jefferies

VIOLENCE IS CAUSED BY . . .

The writing on the walls
The racist people's calls
The drugs that people take
The violence when they wake
The crime that takes place
The punches in the face
The murderers that prowl the roads
That kill people like cars over toads
The violence in the home
Is just like the Colosseum of Rome
The arguments taking place
Right now are all caused by the human race.

Melanie Jane Hickling (17)

GROUND ZERO

The heart of a world lies broken;
 Cold-fractured in one day.
The voice of evil has spoken,
 But just what did it say?
Free-trade's landmark, once distinguished,
 Becomes a concrete tomb,
Innocent lives now extinguished,
 Where ashen shadows loom.
Acrid smoke slow-spirals upward
 From a funeral pyre:
Earth-born souls rising Heavenward,
 Delivered from Hell's fire.
A sky's scarred with sooty bruises
 The sunlight can't defy;
Into my mind shock infuses;
 I ask the question why?
The God I know is peace and love,
 So I can't understand
What vile emotion rules above
Man's care for fellow man?

Wendy R Thomas

NOSTALGIA

Each night in dreams my mind goes back to live again at will
My head is filled with nostalgia
Which crowd around inside my head, I cannot get my fill:
My childhood thoughts, my ambrosia
At night I climb into my bed and close my eyes
My heart settles to a rhythmic beat
I slide gently into a time where no one cries
And again I live in a world elite
My boyhood shouts and the cries of my friends
As I roam with them in the countryside
No sadness dwells in my world where I run about
And live my young life with no need to hide!
Ah! Devon, my Devon where I was reborn
Away from the guns and the bombs of war
Away from the violence where I was torn
Each night from my bed to shelter once more.

Royston E Herbert

THE REASON

Because of all the beauty we have seen
This is the reason the trees are green
Because of all we say and do
This is the reason the sky is blue
Because of all the loneliness we know
This is the reason there is the snow
Because of all the loving pain
This is the reason there is the rain.

Linda Doel

RAINFALL SYMPHONY

Listen to the music, that the raindrops bring,
Listen to the notes, that Mother Nature sings,
During every rainfall, as rhythmic droplets fall to earth,
In a pitter-patter, pitter-patter tune that's full of mirth,
Listen to the birdsong high up in the trees,
As they perch to shelter, beneath the canopies of leaves,
Listen to the crystal pools, resound in harmony,
As ripples dance within them, so happily,
Listen to the pearlized droplets, drumming on the pane,
Listen, and you will hear, the music of the rain.

Clare Allen

AN ELEGY FOR THE INNOCENT

So many have perished for no reason
In the middle of the harvest season.
They were in the wrong place at the wrong time,
That, and that only, was their only crime.
Those who so cravenly slew them may jeer,
But soon they will have little cause to cheer.
We weep for the loss of those innocents
So foully slain, and our innocence
Shattered as surely as the twin towers.
Whilst our rulers and the great powers
Plan the end of the unseen, unknown foe,
Let us mourn the loss of the friends we know
And bring comfort to the tearful bereaved.
And let us think without being deceived,
The struggle to come will be long and hard,
The path will be rough, our passage marred
By doubt, but we will come to haven,
If we be strong, if we be not craven.
But now we must stretch hands across the sea
In token of love's solidarity
To those whose lives have been grimly shattered,
Whose hopes, dreams and very safety battered
By a thunderbolt from out of the blue.
May they have peace of mind, may they renew
In their hearts the blessings of love and hope,
Be they in America or Europe.
May the twin towers rise from the rubble
A symbol of the will to redouble
The endless drive to find peace among men,
The age old quest for the fabled garden.

Ian Holt

CATERPILLAR

Caterpillar climbs up the bark of a tree,
It is such a long climb, he longs to be free,
On to a green leaf is his favourite food,
He munches and munches, its taste is so good.

Is this all there is to this wearisome life?
'Tis where perils abound and dangers are rife,
The birds love little caterpillars to eat,
Such a delicate morsel is quite a treat.

Oh if only he could fly up in the air,
To be light, free and safe, and without a care,
But he is bound to the tree on this dark earth,
'Tis all he has known since the day of his birth.

Caterpillar is ugly, clumsy and slow,
He longs to be beautiful, light and to go,
Flitting through the flowers, dancing round the trees,
Borne upwards and flying around in the breeze.

There's another life he knows nothing about,
A new place in God's kingdom, there is no doubt,
Caterpillar dies as on the tree he clings,
Soon he is borne upwards on gossamer wings.

And so now he is beautiful, light and free,
He flits through the flowers and around the tree,
Where once he was bound and unable to fly,
Pleased he is that to the old life he did die.

So one wonderful day we too shall be free,
If to the Lord Jesus we have bowed the knee,
His precious blood cleanses us from all our sin,
Crucified with Christ, a new life to begin.

Ruth Dewhirst

ONE MOMENT

Just one tiny moment can shatter a day,
Sixty seconds can alter your life.

What started out, as a morning so fine,
Can end in a haze full of strife.

Just ordinary people, going to work,
Their loved ones were left with a kiss.

A thread of destruction, planned far away,
And suddenly, all life is dismissed.

A terrorist plan, has no thought of man,
When seeking his aim just to rule.

A bomb sent a message, and heartache,
And a terrorist vows to be cruel.

It's the luck of the dice, if you'll be there,
It could be your family or me.

When these things keep happening over,
I wonder why God doesn't see.

Duchess Newman

OUTSIDE MAN

Ragged man, in tin-can alleys;
With sore-bone legs; worn-shoe holes;
Spidery hands; garbage-can claws;
Trudging and staggering by closed doors.

Slick gutters; oil-stained puddles;
Cats and vermin; night-time scuffles;
Rotting food; alley-trapped stench;
Mumbling and moaning vagabond wretch.

Hopeless rambling; unsteady steps;
Brown papered bottles; desperate lips;
Corner slumping; saggy dirt face;
The end of his, human race.

Edwin Page

EVACUEE

Long ago when bombs were falling
Seated on a west-bound train
I watched the fields and houses passing
Longing to be home again

Then we stood in trepidation
In a tiny, village hall
Waiting for someone to claim us
Would there be a home for all?

Life seemed slow and very different
From the one that we had known
Primitive by London standards
But the seeds of love were sown

For we found the joys of nature
Helped with jobs about the farm
Searched for wild flowers in the meadow
Away from raids and traffic harm

Gathered mushrooms in the morning
Sandals damp from early dew
Tasted blackberries from the hedgerow
Discovered where the chestnuts grew

Later, with our childhood vanished
We sought again those primrose banks
Found the kindly, ageing people
Expressing our belated thanks

Sheila J Leheup

REAWAKENING

The countryside was looking bleak
the ice got thicker, week by week
and kept at bay the heron's beak.

Small birds were dying by the score
the squirrel could not reach his store
a robin waited at my door.

The season's freezing now has passed
a bird sings on the radio mast
there's blossom on the trees at last.

Jonathan Bryant

THE GARDEN

My garden is a mass of flowers
It cheers up those lonely hours
The colours are blue, pink and red
Pretty lupins beside the shed
Delphiniums, pansies, carnations too
From the window a lovely view
Blackbirds nesting in the hedge
A baby perched upon the ledge
Pigeons cooing upon the roof
A strange bird that stands aloof
Seagulls screeching as they fly
Large white wing span in the sky
A cat miaows and lies in wait
Poor little bird could meet its fate
In the pond swim the fish
For the cat - a tasty dish!
I chase it - stopping it at prey
It will return another day
In the summer this is the scene
Sky is blue - grass is green
Come the winter, when it is cold
The frost will keep the plants on hold
Earth will be hard - the pond will be froze
If you venture out Jack Frost nips the nose
Spring brings more colour, crocus in bloom
Helps us forget the darkness and gloom
Nature is wonderful, giving us pleasure
So amazing, too hard to measure

E Wakeford

STEAMY WINDOWS

I can feel your body stirring gently in the early morning hush,
I can feel the breathings from your body rush.
Your hands reach for me gently drawing my body in
Touching all my senses and the wanting within.
My body yields towards you and we both become one,
Engulfed with tender feelings before the early morning sun.
My heart gives in completely; I can feel your every touch
Steamy windows in the bedroom, blocks out any light as such.
We are totally oblivious to anything around,
It's you and me completely in the love we've both found.
You to me are special and I'm surrounded by a mist,
And it all starts when I surrender to your warm and tender kiss.

Vera Margaret Collins

IN REMEMBRANCE OF SALLY

Remember seeing the advert, good home wanted for Red Setter,
Remember the apprehension before we went to get her.
Remember how she shook with fear when we put her in the car,
Remember just how sick she was, the journey was quite far.
Remember too how thin she was, she stole some food that night,
Remember meals five times a day to put that factor right.
Remember the only thing she knew, that Sally was her name,
Remember it was not our choice, but we kept it just the same.
Remember hours of training her to sit, lie down and stay,
Remember hours of fun with her, oh how she loved to play.
Remember all her gentle ways, her eyes of liquid brown,
Remember how we trusted her, she never let us down.
Remember how the children lay down by her side,
Remember we could not scold her, not that we really tried.
Remember how we watched her slowly growing old,
Remember how we loved her, Sally with heart of gold.
Remember that sad morning, knowing the best thing for our friend
Was to hold her gently in our arms and let her suffering end.
Remember carrying her outside and burying her by the tree,
To be remembered always in our hearts, our lovely dog Sally.

Margaret Fisher

CANADA'S QUEST

Come, journey with me, take my hand
Across Canada's fair and distant land
Come, journey with me on nature's quest
From the north, south, east to west
Atlantic giants, humpback and minke
Tail, sail and dive, then gently sink
Polar bears gather in Hudson Bay
When the thaw arrives they swim away
Blizzards of seabirds, hear their cry
Majestic icebergs glide on by
The northern lights, a spectacular sight
Vivid colours illuminate the skies at night
Caribou roam in the north-west territories
Elk and wolves and the mighty grizzlies
The Rocky Mountains canyons so deep
Klondike, Goldrush at Dawson Creek
Quaint little places like Medicine Hat
Beautiful lakes like Whisky Jack
Fundy Bay, Heron Bay, Cloud Bay too
Thunder Bay, Echo Bay to name but a few
North American Indians grace this special place
Visit their reservations, observe their sacred ways
Respect this land and see nature at its best
Enjoy life's journey as you take Canada's quest.

Barbara M Ward-Schmitz

NIGHT INTO DAY

I stole a fragment of the night
A shade of deepest black,
And then I carefully placed it
Inside a small velvet sack.

The years past and I forgot my prize
And even where it lay,
The velvet fabric rotted
And the night burst into day.

I was swept aside by the darkness
It grew and grew, spreading over the earth,
I wondered how I might stop it
For I had been the cause of its birth.

It spread over land and sea
Until its texture became so fine
It split into a myriad pieces
And with each object it did entwine.

But I need not have worried
For I had only created shadows
Yet he that steals that which is God's
What he unleashes no one knows.

Jack Ellis

I WISH

I wish that I could write a line to help somebody else.
I wish that I could find the rhyme expressive of myself
That someone else would recognise and say, 'That's how I feel,
I never knew that poetry could reflect what's truly real!'

Just the thought, that what I say, holds meaning for another
Makes me strive to get it right; show feelings I would cover.
And when I've sought elusive words I hope that they will find
And bring alive, in someone else, the thoughts upon my mind.

If talent's there, will it shine through, or do I waste my time?
Try too hard for meanings, hoping desperately to rhyme!
If I could make a literary mark upon this earth
Would it be erased, or might it stand and have a little worth?

Rose Stedman

A CHANGE OF MIND

Through the house fast footfalls echoed:
Outside, dawn broke and a cock crowed;
Yet, within, no one stirred and through
Broken casements a raw wind blew -

And by the gate
A battered board
Still hung like bait
Although ignored
Now except by
Those who knew not
The reason why
'Twas left to rot -

That rambling, melancholy house
Whose nameplate bore just one word: 'Faust';
Whose rafters, ceilings, floors and walls
Whispered warped hints of Hades' halls -

And no one came
A second time
To view: its shame
Bored deep, like grime
Engrained. As light
To darkness flowed
In ceaseless flight
Footfalls echoed -

As if someone strove to evade
Some consequence: some pact they'd made.

Diane Elizabeth Maltby

A DAY AT THE BEACH

Sandwiches are made
We've a bucket and spade
Cream for the bugs
Towels and rugs
We are going for the day to the sea
My friends all say rather you than me

Memories of when the children were small
A day on the beach for one and all
A shivering child, sand stuck to the skin
Fresh clothes on, then they are soaking
Sandwiches and sand
We forgot the armbands
Don't walk with your shoes into the sea
Ice creams are dripping
They are not for licking
Eat them up fast
Or they will not last

Keep your hat on your head
Or you'll end up in bed
I'd rather you kept your T-shirt on
No, please don't play around groyne
Pick up our bits
The sea's crept in
The kids are in fits
At the raucous scene

We have settled again
No the clouds don't mean rain
Let's have coffee to keep up our strength
Oh that breeze is heaven sent

A M Seago

THE CHRISTMAS KITTEN

Asked to write about this time,
Dismay, nostalgia intertwine.
The culture, friends and tinselled tree,
Warm feelings absent here for me.

Then the Christmas kitten walked in,
Fresh and innocent,
Guiltless of blood,
Ready and willing to play.

Gracious gifts from aged aunts,
Emigrants and confidantes.
Thought considered, launched her ship
On a distant level sea.
Ripples echoed overhead,
The yearly swing from thee to me.

Food, music, friendship, gifts,
Senses fill, expectations lift.
Why?
Why bother?

A charade of commercial tat,
Good taste scoffs at all of that.
Flat and useless splurge,
Leaks onward from the twenty-third.

Then the Christmas kitten walked in
Fresh and innocent,
Guiltless of blood,
Ready and willing to play.

O child look up,
The black night slides away.
And from the clouds
Bright stars you'll pluck,
For joy, this Christmas day.

Margaret Sellars

BELLY BIGOT

Give us a clue, no give us a treat,
Let me guess what you're like from the things you eat,
Go for the quiche or go for baked beans,
Any student of food can see what that means,
Is your food kind, or is your food cruel,
Or is eating to you simply taking on fuel,
Talk about food or talk about drink,
But I hope what you do eat can make you think.

Jim Riley

DAYS LIKE THESE

It's days like these, I need you
Nobody else could ever do
A teardrop falls
My lonely heart calls

It's days like these, I need you more
When I keep looking at the door
Your touch, your words, your gentle kiss
There's nothing about you I don't miss

It's days like these, I want you here
When the day begins to disappear
When the night begins to fall
Once again my lonely heart begins to call

Amanda Steel

LAUGHING OR PURRING

Sweetness may be an honest thing,
But no more feline than a king.
Many smug smiles have licked this thought,
If paws could write, and cats would talk.

If they less enjoyed the towering trees,
Tails swishing swiftly in the breeze.
And we know not the reason why,
It's more fun to chase a butterfly,
Or listen to the shadows talk
Where us mere mortals fear to walk.

But to the cat who only loves the moon,
Our mindless world will not change quite soon;
And were they human and all feline thoughts were true,
Why, each cat would live to be a genius too!

Joanne Wheeler

A Jury's Right

Walking along the paved street,
A policeman smiled, looked so neatly dressed.
An early conscious man on the beat,
It is Hutton HQ he wishes to impress.

Making notes in his notepad
He sees a robbery in the distance
Handcuff those men and the superintendent will be glad
Nothing will stop me with my persistence.

All recorded and witnesses at the station
The villains have the access into court
The jail offers a toilet in the corner for his pollution
A mate the villain meets of his own sort.

Tap, tap, tap goes the hammer
All rise in respect to the judge
Give him 20 years in the slammer
For no more will he ever budge.

Heather Edwards

THE LETTER AND THE DIAMOND KEYS

(For my Mother)

I dreamt I found a golden bottle
on a far off distant beach
many miles did it tumble
travel me to reach

Carried by torrents
current and sea breeze
inside a letter and
a bunch of diamond keys

I opened the golden bottle
and in my eye a snow-white crystal tear
expecting words of wisdom
some teaching from a seer

I scoured the paper thorough
both sides my eyes did scan
but not a word was written
'twas empty as a Klondyke pan

By now my heart was broken
I fell trembling to my knees
then in the perfect mauve of midnight
I felt the diamond keys

But no lock had I
for my diamond keys to fit
just miles of sand, endless skies
and a tattered poet's kit

So sadly I did fall asleep
in my dream within a dream
I dreamt of stars, flowers and fishes
in their stream

Alas the morn did wake me
it woke me with a start
my letter and my diamond keys
were resting on my heart

Now the moral of my tale
is not to teach or cure
it's just that when your hopes seem certain
at first you must be sure

S Feerick
(Lamb)

SECURITY GUARD

S ite on, log on with faithful hound
E erie sounds, no one around
C oming of dusk, light fading, air cool
U nited we stand, divided we fall
R oaming the site, torch in hand
I lluminating the night sky from the land
T ime dragging slowly, way by it drift
Y earning for the end of the shift

G uarding all with all your might
U nveiling shadow of the night
A larm switch light flashing red
R ain or sun, onward you tread
D reaming of a nice, cosy, warm bed.

P Brewer

THE SEA

Where has the sea's colour gone?
It cannot be for lack of the sun,
Because the year has only just begun.
Where has the sea's colour gone?

Nicola Barnes

THE NEW PLAYER

Our football team never did very much
we had me and Bill, Earl and Butch.
And our school team always were beat,
until this player moved to our street.

This player moved in from across the Tyne
with a football brain - ever so fine.
This player plays 'striker' most match days
and outruns us all with incredible pace.

This player never bungles a tackle or charge
no matter the player, no matter how large.
And this player is friendly - and always polite
never yells or spits or starts a fight.

We were playing league 'champs' only last week
who were trying to break our winning streak.
With a minute to go with one goal each
this player scored a goal that was such a 'peach'.

A few of the players and their parents say
they don't believe this player should play
but she's good as me, Bill, Butch and Earl,
so we don't care - that the kid is a girl.

Alex Branthwaite

IN MY HUMBLE OPINION

In my humble opinion, this love thing's not that great!
True love makes you its minion, its bondslave date-by-date!
It seems to me, you compromise, yet love, itself, won't bend!
At times I've wondered, full of whys. The questions never end.
And yet I've fallen for its tricks, its whimsies on the way.
It's only when I'm 'knocked for six' with daydreams that I'll play.
But now I know its repertoire, its gambits and its rules,
I'll not join in its mad hoorah like billions of other fools!
I'd rather live with loneliness than play the game as is.
At least your heart's not in a mess tormented by true bliss!
Love is a drug, a fantasy, the best of all your hopes,
And yet no guard 'gainst misery when you're left on the ropes!
When crucified by day and night by all each sigh creates,
Then love will only watch you fight the fury of the fates!
You'll see I'm right, you'll understand. Roulette is much more kind!
For love will lead you by the hand then let you lose your mind!
Seek not its treasures and rewards. Your soul should not be bought!
Love's the fakir, the king of frauds! Stay wise and don't get caught!
Walk past all beauty in your path - ignore all offers given!
Then you will have the final laugh on leaving Earth for Heaven . . .

D K F Martindale

THE VASE OF ROSES

Once stood a vase of brightly coloured roses
Full of life and sprightly spirited poses.
Positioned just right for all to see
The blooms seemed to call to me.

Such dashing beauty there on show
Jaunty colours with flare and glow.
Some were in bud, others in bloom
They provided such aura in the room.

But something happened, just for a while
The vase of beauty turned volatile.
What made such beauty turn so erratic?
From the first extreme that was so erotic.

It seemed for a while that they would demise
But the beauty was enough to suffice.
As it seemed that they would wilt
They appeared to sing a kind of lilt.

They lifted their heads in a boastful fashion
As if suddenly filled with lustful passion.
Once again stands the vase in bloom
Looking as peppery and effervescent again in the room.

Michaela W Moore

SHE!

Involving, puzzle solving, intending to rule,
Impressive, possessive - she is nobody's fool,
Embracing, she is facing an outlook supreme,
Like pudding, she's looking to be more than the cream,
A temper will help her to understand,
None cuter a future for her we have planned,
Unsteady, puts her teddy at the forefront of the scene,
Delightful, an eyeful, on controlling she is keen,
No other, this mother, she does so impress,
Constructive, destructive, the place is in a mess,
Rewarding, still hoarding and does sometimes cry,
So becoming, her plumbing cannot control but she'll try,
So much fun, life has begun - a long way to go,
My possession, it's my confession, wonderful to know,
Must get the seating, always eating - she never is full,
She's all mine, absolutely divine - someone wonderful,
Must get going, she's so knowing, knows it's time for her food,
What of tomorrow, will another follow to add to the brood,
Life's tough, is she enough - should our loving cease?
Would another, perhaps a brother - disrupt our peace?
She's demanding, commanding, must stop chatting to you now,
See she's coming, blast that plumbing - the potty again makes its bow,
Cannot fault her, glad we sought her, must mop up the water,
She is mine, so divine, my first born baby daughter!

John L Wright

DESPAIR AND HOPE

Jet-black coal on an unlit fire.
Shadows passing through her mind.
A starless sky, an endless mire,
was she ever peace to find?

Dull and grey the morning.
Metallic clouds, a leaden sky.
Sombre clouds with the dawning
of this day - the long goodbye.

Colours trapped within her mind,
vacuuming her sense of loss.
An inner strength somewhere to find.
Before her she sees a rugged cross.

Dapple horses tall and proud
taking him to eternal rest,
encased within wrapped in his shroud,
her love, her life - the final test.

Clouds shining silver above an inky grave.
Consolation now doth start.
Light filtering in, its way to pave
each corner of her heavy heart.

Morning dawns fresh and new.
Her mind now calm, no longer wild.
He is at peace, as she is too,
and within her womb stirs his child.

Josie Rawson

HEART OF COLD

Your eyes seer heartlessly through the poem,
Like a dagger thrust from title to nom be plume.
Would you do likewise were these words your own,
You're a critic's critic may I boldly assume?

Yes, these words were written with bohemian blood,
From an austere existence out of want and need!
As your caustic drivel dries up the flood,
Then you stand and watch the poet bleed.

Hugh S McKay

DEADLY RAGWORT

A handsome plant with golden yellow flowers
Blooming in July despite the thunder showers,
Its flowers turn neglected acres into seas of gold
Ragwort a flower of beauty to behold.
Insects and butterflies upon its nectar feed
Yet farmers despise it as a dangerous weed,
For if this plant by horse or cow consumed
Due to its toxins then their lives are doomed.
How strange that flowers of ragwort, beauteous to the eyes
Distract us from this lethal killer in disguise.

David A Garside

ANOTHER SONG

A bell may hang in a spire and not ring,
A cat may eat a nightingale, yet not sing,
A versifier may aspire and has a tongue
To condemn the one who killed the lively song:
That bird's tune will not return,
But of the poet's anguish may be born
A mellifluous poem to sweeten nights,
And chasten cats with lowly appetites.

Mary Frances Mooney

THE FRIENDLY DRAGON

I'd lie there trying to go to sleep
But every now and then I'd peep
My mother beside me on the bed
I'd listen to the story she read.

The tale began, there was this wood
Mysterious, dark and scary,
Inside the undergrowth a dragon stood
And on his back a fairy.

The dragon looked so very sad,
As he wandered through the trees,
How could he scare and be so bad,
When he could not even sneeze.

'I'm big and green and full of scales,
Yet not like a dragon in the fairy tales,'
The fairy smiled and stroked his back.
'It's only fire that you lack.

Anyway, I'd like to say,
People prefer you just that way.'
A smile appeared upon his face,
He tried to hide his true disgrace.

Then a bee came buzzing about,
Flying up the dragon's snout,
The dragon roared this eerie sound,
Spitting the bee out on the ground.

In anger the dragon gave a puff,
And there were flames, sure enough,
The bee fled away in utter despair,
The fairy gasped, the dragon stared.

'Was that me?' he said with glee,
Fairy laughed, 'Who else could it be?'
Now the dragon is full of laughter,
And so they lived happily ever after.

J Roberts

MENTAL BLOCK

My mind is not working the way that it should,
The poems that come out are not very good,
But my rhymes are all hard and in a big mess,
And what I write, I could not care less,
It's not depression but disinterest,
So where are all the words that I can harvest,
I need something to set my mind in motion,
Something to give it a good thought or notion,
Something to set it a bit of a tingle,
Many words and phrases to sit and mingle,
And now my brain is in a bit of a tizz,
It's starting to germinate, bubble and fizz,
But how long will it take to get it right,
Maybe an hour or a day or a night,
I hope it comes quickly, it's getting a pain,
Oh! What is happening, I can not explain,
And now words are gelling, starting to form, rhyme,
In my mind running, skipping, like in a mime,
Like water they come, quickly flow upon flow,
Now my mind is happy, it's starting to glow.

Nicolette A Thomas

REGAN OUR SETTER

You came to us just six weeks old, a silky red bundle of joy
And when you met our Labrador you played him up, oh boy
You chased his tail, you bit his ear and gave him so much hassle
As time went by and he grew old yet he was king of the castle
He soon had to go to his long rest so you gave us consolation
Your nutty ways and Irish wit with loyalty and dedication
A nature so friendly that would melt a heart of stone
You only had the best of food and could never tackle a bone
When your meal was over from the kitchen you would saunter
To wipe your face on any guest, not knowing you shouldn't oughta
Like burnished copper was your coat, it shone and was so soft
You had a very noble stance and held your head aloft
You're now fifteen yet very brave, it's difficult to walk
We know what you would say if only you could talk
So goodbye my wonderful, faithful friend, I'm sure we'll meet again
Somehow, somewhere, one never knows, but 'twill not be the end

June Jefferson

WINTER'S SNOW

Whiteness covers the houses and the streets
Deep and crisp and cold to the feet
Fingers tingle as they try to keep warm
The snow has lain deep from early dawn

This beauty that lies in country and town
Has all bewitched with its gentle sound
Even the night has a glow of its own
With this blanket of soft, winter's snow

Journeys are made no matter how hard
As every cold inch measures a yard
Feet sink deeply in white surround
Trying to find their way to the ground

Each step can be fun but also a task
Knowledge gives strength to know it won't last
In each situation someone finds joy
To children who play, the snow is a toy

Fires will be built to last for the night
Cosy rooms bathe in bright embers of light
Little ones cuddle with all of their might
Noses and toes kept well out of sight

This Christmas will be one to hold dear
With friends and family and holiday cheer
Somehow this mantle of winter snow
Gives to all hearts a warm season's glow

Gillian Mullett

A FISHY BUSINESS

Last night, a ton of wet fish was delivered to my door.
It is an unsightly vision that I would rather just ignore.
How can you stand there with that look upon your face?
You can forget the blessed smirk right now or I'll smack you
                                                    with a plaice.

For five and twenty years we've been going on like this.
You take your life with a pinch of salt and a pint you'll never miss.
I wait around for closing time with the sleeping blanket on,
At half-past twelve you're still not home and all my passion's gone.

Men and boys are all the same with their don't care attitude.
It's work and wash and watch the box and then 'Woman,
                                        where's mi food!'
They burp and belch to finish the meal, their waists are far too tight,
And then it's time for bed and sleep before they've said 'Goodnight'.

Last night, a ton of wet fish was delivered to my door.
Or maybe is it just that I didn't notice it before?
The reality of life is a pain sometimes to face.
Shall I ask him to do the decent thing and smack me with a plaice?

Sudha Patrick